1987

Show Me How:
A Manual for Parents of Preschool Visually Impaired and Blind Children

Mary Brennan, M.S. Ed.

Mary Brennan is Director of Weekend College,
Dominican College, Orangeburg, N. Y. 10913.

AFB Practice Reports
Published by the American Foundation for the Blind
15 West 16th Street, New York, N. Y. 10011

Table of Contents

Foreword

"It is one of the most beautiful compensations of life that no man can sincerely try to help another without helping himself."

— Ralph Waldo Emerson

The author of this manual experienced the reality of Emerson's "beautiful compensation" in the contribution of her ideas, perceptions, and observations gathered and developed in working with blind and visually impaired preschoolers.

This manual is addressed primarily to parents, teachers and teacher's assistants, but will be of value to all those involved in the growth and development of preschoolers. The activities and exercises described herein offer specific procedures and activities which serve as a practical guide to the attainment of goals set for the child.

Mary Dean Brennan's contributions are the result of her professional experience as well as her enthusiasm and creativity in working with blind and visually impaired youngsters. Her efforts will help others develop a like enthusiasm and an informed response to the needs and opportunities presented during this important stage of learning and growth. The means to achievement of successful work with blind and visually impaired preschoolers are within the grasp of those who read this manual.

— Sr. Mary McCormick
Dominican College
Orangeburg, New York

Preface

Parents of a blind or visually handicapped child often feel that they and their child have suffered a dreadful loss. Parents will be anxious about their child's future and worry that a person with such a handicap will literally live in a world of darkness, unable to get around or fend for himself.

It's important to remember that this sense of loss is the parents' alone. Your child does not feel any sense of loss and is completely unaware that he is handicapped. And he's basically right: your blind or visually impaired child is much more like sighted children than he is different from them. His needs are the same: to be cuddled and cooed at, bounced and played with, and, above all, included as a member of the family. Like all other children, he can experience the joys of growing and learning, of loving and being loved.

Your child will react to his handicap the way he senses that you do. Your attitude toward his visual impairment will probably become his attitude. You can use this manual to help develop your child's abilities to the fullest. As you work with him, your own confidence in his abilities will probably increase, and your strengthened confidence will be communicated to your child.

If your child has some limited amount of vision (such a person is often referred to as "partially sighted," "visually impaired," or "visually handicapped") encourage him to use it. As you read this manual, choose the activities best suited for your blind or partially sighted child. This manual is intended primarily for preschoolers with no handicap other than blindness or visual impairment.

Only you as parent of a handicapped child can know the feelings that come with this experience. I cannot lessen the intensity of that feeling nor can I offer any easy solutions. My hope is that you will take the time to step back and think about what has been written for you on the following pages and that it may be a source of help.

A manual of this nature is not possible without the help and encouragement of a lot of friends and relatives. To all of you, I express my heartfelt thanks. Special thanks: to the precious little children of the Headstart programs, whose unique way of helping each other planted the idea for writing this manual; to their parents, whose frustrations and anxieties prompted me to write it; to my husband, Jack, who read the manuscript patiently and gave me the gentle challenge to finish it; and most especially to Sr. Mary McCormick, whose magnanimous spirit and personal dedication to the field of special education has been a source of strength and inspiration to the many teachers of the visually impaired who have been fortunate enough to have had her as a mentor and friend.

M. D. B.

Chapter 1

Signposts to Growing and Learning

There is no such person as a typical blind or visually impaired child. Each is an individual. Each has his own needs which are special to him. You, as a parent, must develop the strength to deal with these needs. In the months following birth, the bonds of affection and attachment will start forming.

Do not be afraid to talk about your feelings. As one mother described it: "It would be unrealistic for me to say that I was not sad, scared, and sorry. I cried a lot. I did not know what to do or how to do it." Her advice: "Do not hide your feelings: Ask questions and ask for help."

It is hard to hide your feelings from the people you live with. Talk to your husband, your children, and any other people directly in contact with your son or daughter. Remember that they are also experiencing some of the same feelings. Ask your doctor or local school to give you the name of someone who works with blind and visually impaired children. Counseling may help to air many of the thoughts that you have not been able to say to any member of the family.

You don't have to be taught how to be a mother or father; this will come naturally once your baby is in your arms. Maintain a loving manner towards your son or daughter and others will follow your lead. They will come to understand your child's abilities as well as the limitations imposed by his handicap.

A blind child must depend upon his other senses to learn things. Therefore it is very important that you as a parent do not become too helpful. Allow him the freedom to explore under your loving, watchful eye. Let him find out about his surroundings by using his own clues. Be there if he gets stuck or needs a question answered. Remember to be protective, not over-protective. Give your child the same opportunities to grow and learn that you would give his sighted brother or sister.

Individual growth starts at birth and continues day by day. For the blind child, his environment and family play the most important role in his development. Give him the companionship of his family, exploit the opportunities afforded by his environment, and build his confidence by encouraging him to try new things. Be realistic in what you expect your child to accomplish, praise him for what he can do, and be patient about what he cannot do. Be sincere and honest in your actions and attitudes. Remember that the blind child is sensitive to people's true feelings. Rest assured that mistakes you make will be more than compensated for by true love and affection.

This chapter is divided into suggested activities, observations and notes. The activities are grouped according to age. Each objective has a "success achieved" line so that you as the parent-teacher can tell if and when you have finished with that particular activity. Each activity will vary in the amount of time it will take for your child to learn. Be patient and loving and success will come naturally. The observations are included so that you will be aware of that particular action or activity. The notes are added to explain why some materials are better than others or should be used in a different manner.

Suggestions for
the First Year

0 to 4 months

Objective: To develop a smile.
Procedure: Begin by handling the baby often during each day, especially at times other than feeding and bathing. Gently cradling and touching the baby should make him smile. Talk to him as you play with him, and sing soft songs.

Success is achieved when the baby smiles when touched, and ultimately responds with a smile when he hears your voice.

Objective: To encourage head control.
Procedure: When holding your baby, talk with your cheek next to his to encourage him to raise his head.

When the baby is lying on his stomach, call him and get him to turn his head.

Place your child lying on his stomach over a pillow or over your knee and stimulate him to lift his head by stroking or tickling the back of his neck. In this same position, gently raise one shoulder at a time forcing him to support his weight on his arms.

Place your child on his back with his head on a cushion and encourage him to reach forward with his arms as you shake a rattle in front of him. If need be, place his fingers on his toes. This will help him to go forward.

Success is achieved when you can see that he can lift his head and control the way he holds it.

Objective: To encourage rolling from back to stomach.
Procedure: Place your baby's head on a cushion, then hold one arm up beside his head and roll his head over this arm toward the floor; hips and opposite arm will follow.

Roll one leg over the other, rolling the baby's hips and his head will follow.

Repeat these procedures daily and often.

Success is achieved when baby rolls over by himself.

5 to 6 months

Objective: To develop movements of hands and arms toward an object.
Procedure: Place a mobile made of rattles, toys with bells and chewable items across the crib. Let it hang low enough that the baby can hit it, making a noise. Take his hands and go through the motion of playing with it; hit the bell and rattle.

Success is achieved when your baby reaches toward the toys by himself.

7 to 8 months

Objective: To reach out for an object when it is dropped.
Procedure: Place a rattle or other noise-making toy in your baby's hand. Let it drop and then put his hand through the movements of finding the dropped toy. Repeat daily and often.

Success is achieved when your baby begins to reach out for an object such as a rattle when it is dropped from his hands.

Objective: To sit up with support for several minutes.
Procedure: Prop the baby up in the corner of a couch or upholstered chair using pillows

for support if necessary. Let him sit in this new position for a few minutes. Gently talk with him.

Success is achieved when the baby is able to sit for three minutes and not fall over or cry to be moved.

Observation: Sometimes at seven months, your baby will react and cry when a stranger comes near him or picks him up. Try to have a stranger hold him while the mother is present. The baby will sense by the tone of the mother's voice how she feels toward the stranger and this will help the baby to relax.

9 to 11 months

Objective: To develop coordination of hearing and feeling.
Procedure: Hold a rattle in your hand and shake it over the baby's head. Try to get him to reach toward the sound. If he does not, put his hands up and let him shake the rattle. Repeat the procedures often. Change the location and the toy used once you think he may be losing interest.

Success is achieved when the baby reaches out and touches the rattle or the bell.

Objective: To develop crawling.
Procedure: Place clocks, radios, or music boxes at various spots on the floor and call to your baby to come to the music. Let him know that you are close by talking to him as often as necessary. If you see that he does not know what to do, kneel over him and move his hands and knees as if he were crawling. Practice crawling with your eyes closed so that you will be saying the right directions. Do this exercise at least twice daily.

Success is achieved when your baby crawls to the source of the sound and touches it.

Objective: To have the baby pull himself to a standing position and lower himself to a sitting one.
Procedure: Place your baby alongside a table which is sturdy and secured to the floor so that it will not fall over when the baby leans on it. Talk with him and try to get him to place his hands on the table and pull himself up as you give him directions. If there is no response, manipulate his body and then pull him up by placing your hands under his armpits and gently standing him up. Repeat the procedure until he gets the idea of what it means to stand and sit.

Success is achieved when your baby pulls himself up alone and then sits down.

Observation: At this age your baby will imitate the sounds he hears. Play a game and make whatever sound he makes; then change it by making everyday sounds like a bell ringing, a clock ticking and a fire engine clanging. Try to get him to repeat them after you. Do not leave music playing all the time. After a while, this becomes mere noise and he will begin to ignore it and other sounds. He can't close his ears. If possible, tape record his own sounds and play them back to him.

12 to 14 months

Objective: To drink from a cup or glass, helping to hold it.
Procedure: Place the child's hands on the cup and your hand over his, raise the cup to his lower lip and tell him to take a little into his mouth and swallow it. Repeat the procedure often every day.

Success is achieved when your child can drink without your having to say, "take a drink."

Objective: To stand alone and walk forward by himself.

3

Procedure: To help your child take his first steps alone, have two adults sit opposite each other about two feet apart; stand the child up by one of the adults and have the other one talk to him and encourage him to walk to him while holding both of his hands. Gradually increase the space between the two adults and decrease the amount of physical support—hold only one hand, and then prompt him to walk alone. Encourage your child to go from one to the other by clapping or talking to him.

Success is achieved when your child is able to walk alone without holding hands with anyone.

Objective: To give you a toy when asked.

Procedure: Using a toy that he is familiar with, ask him to give it to you. Take his hand and show him what the words "give to me" mean.

Success is achieved when your child is able to give a toy to you when you say, "Please give it to me."

Observation: Nursery equipment at this age can include: rattles, spools, wrist balls, toys with bells, canvas swing, playpen, rocking horse, squeaky toys, rubber blocks, tin cups, small cans without sharp edges.

Note: Care must be taken when using a playpen. Your child should not be confined to a small space all the time. He needs to crawl around and explore. Use the playpen as a spot where you can safely leave your child when you cannot watch him. When he is in the playpen give him some of his toys or interesting things like pots and pans to play with.

14 to 16 months

Objective: To search for and locate dropped objects.

Procedure: Standing next to your child, drop a rattle and ask him to find it. Then place the rattle in his hand and have him drop it and then bend over to find it. If he is unable to do it, use a music box or a loud ticking clock so that he will be able to follow the sound as it hits the floor and locate it.

Success is achieved when he can drop and find an object by himself.

Objective: To increase coordination.

Procedure: Place two bells in a paper bag and have the child carry it into another room.

Each morning, have your child put his dirty clothes in a basket or hamper located in another room.

At meal times, have your child put little things, like salt and pepper, mustard, or ketchup on the table.

Success is achieved when he can carry the objects to the correct place without dropping them.

16 to 24 months

Be patient during this time and keep a washcloth handy!

Objective: To pick up a glass and put it back on the table.

Procedure: Place his hands on the glass. Stand behind him and place your hands over his. Together pick up the glass and have him take a drink from it and then put it back on the table. Fill the glass only a little. Repeat often each day.

Success is achieved when your child can pick up the glass and put it back on the table without your help.

Objective: To eat with a spoon.

Procedure: Fill a bowl with a few Cheerios. Sing a little song: dip, slide and into the mouth; dip, slide and into the mouth.

While standing behind him, move his hand into the bowl as if you were going to spoon out some Cheerios. Repeat the actions a few times, then place the spoon in his hand and have him grasp it tightly. Now move his hand through the action making sure he gets some Cheerios on the spoon. Repeat the action a few times. On each attempt make sure he completes the action by placing a few of the Cheerios in his mouth.

Success is achieved when your child is able to feed himself.

Note: You may find it helpful at the begining to use a square dish with high sides. This will help to lessen the amount of cereal that is pushed over the side.

Objective: To learn about stairs.
Procedure: Allow the child to explore the stairs. Let him sit on them, lie down on them, and feel how big they are. After this is done walk up the entire flight with him, turn and come down. Tell him what they are made of and why there is a handrail, if there is one.

Success is achieved when your child lifts his foot to climb when he comes to the first stop at the bottom.

Objective: To encourage him to say what he wants and needs.
Procedure: At meals, do not fill his glass with any drink; let him ask for some milk. Fill a little and have him ask for more when he wants more. This approach can be used with many different foods at meals or toys during playtime.

Success is achieved when the child realizes he can ask for and get the food and drink he wants.

Objective: To have the child begin to play with other children.
Procedure: If he has siblings, this will happen naturally. If not, invite other children over for milk and cookies. Give the other children a simple explanation of his blindness. Children are very understanding and accepting. If they have a question they will ask it. Provide toys that they can all play with.

Success is achieved if the child does not withdraw or become hostile with the other children.

24 to 36 months
Objective: To encourage standing and walking independently.
Procedure: Set your child's toys out on a low table. This will force him to stand to play. Use a harness to support him as he stands if he is still unsteady. This will improve his balance by allowing him the freedom to use his arms.

Take the child outdoors and let him walk on different surfaces like grass and gravel so that he will get used to them.

Carry your child only when he is too tired to walk.

Success is achieved when the child is able to walk from one spot to another by himself.

Suggestions for
the Third Year

Objective: To encourage responsibility.
Procedure: After returning from the grocery store, have your child help in putting away

the groceries. His job may be to put all the paper goods in the closet. Other areas of responsibility might be to water the plants or feed any pets.

Success is achieved when the child can do the job without any assistance.

Objective: To learn to button and unbutton.

Procedure: Using large buttons and button holes, have your child, with your help, slip the button through the hole. Repeat the procedure a few times. Then while giving directions, let him try to button and then unbutton by himself.

Success is achieved when the child can button and unbutton without assistance.

Objective: To encourage listening skills.

Procedure: Take a walk and talk about the sounds you hear. Have him point to the direction from which they are coming. Play a game in which he points and you see if you can guess the sound he has just heard coming from that direction. Concentrate on normal, everyday sounds like cars, trucks, birds, planes, etc.

Success is achieved when he can correctly point to where a sound is coming from.

Objective: To encourage independence in self-care skills.

Procedure: Put up low hooks for his clothes in the hall and for his towel in the bathroom. Show him how and where to hang up his things. Repeat daily.

Success is achieved when your child hangs up his things without being told to do so.

Observation: Blind children welcome a routine. This is a good age to start one if you have not done so yet. He will find security in knowing that his things will be in the same place. If you must change a routine, do so, but tell him why and how it is going to be different.

Suggestions for the Fourth Year

Objective: To learn how to jump.

Procedure: Ask your child to jump off a low step or a block while you hold his hands. Tell him or move him to bend his knees to get the feel of springing or jumping. Repeat frequently.

Success is achieved when he can jump from a step by himself.

Objective: To learn to hop.

Procedure: Hold his hand, ask him to move his feet to stand on one leg, bend his knee and then bounce up and down. Once he learns the motion, have him hop over a book or a box.

Success is achieved when he can hop three times on both feet, then lift the right leg and hop on the left foot and then, lift the left leg and hop on the right foot.

Objective: To learn the functions of various household appliances.

Procedure: Using toy equipment, your child can learn the function of many appliances: vacuum cleaners, for instance.

Success is achieved when your child is able to tell you what the appliance is used for: Example: a vacuum cleaner picks up dirt.

Objective: To increase hand strength.

Procedure: Encourage your child to play with sponge balls, play dough, clay and sponges in water. Play finger games with your child, such as, "Itsy-bitsy spider" and "Where is thumbkin?"

Encourage rough and tumble play, also wheel-barrow races. Take a rope and have a tug-of-war game.

Success is achieved when you can feel a pull from your child's end of the rope.

Suggestions: This is a good time for nursery school or Sunday school. Also invite children to come over and play with your child. Serve cookies and milk, and provide interesting toys to play with. Begin teaching your child limits; tell him that he must not cross the street by himself nor play near the curb areas.

Suggestions for
the Fifth Year

Objective: To create with his hands.
Procedure: Place string and beads on a table. String a few beads with him until he is able to do it by himself. Encourage him to make a present for a relative or a friend.

Success is achieved when he completes the necklace and gives it to the person.

Objective: To learn how to run.
Procedure: Using a baton or lightweight stick, have the child place two hands on it. Place one of your hands on the same stick so that you can hold it and tilt it up for a right hand turn and down for a left hand turn. By holding it straight you are telling your child that you are going to run straight ahead. Run in a park, in the street, or anywhere there is room.

Success is achieved when your child is able to run in the correct direction without having to be told which way he is going.

Objective: To promote language development.
Procedure: Pick a favorite nursery rhyme and have your child act out one of the characters. Example, the wolf in the *Three Little Pigs*.

Success is achieved when he can use words rather than actions to tell his version of the story.

Objective: To encourage responsibility.
Procedure: Talk together about different things that have to be done every day around the house. Encourage him to pick one job that he will be responsible for every day. Set up a system where he will be rewarded for remembering and doing "his job." Be sure the reward is agreed to by both you and your child.

Success is achieved when he does his job and receives his reward.

Suggestions: Encourage him to enter into all family conversations. Provide opportunities in which he can succeed and receive praise. Let him play with mud, finger paints, play dough and modeling clay.

Chapter 2

Building A
Self-Concept

You will quickly learn that the needs of your blind child are similar to those of a sighted child. As parents you will provide the stimulation necessary to encourage him to develop his natural gifts to the fullest. You will do this spontaneously without prompting. You can help form a positive self-image for your child by giving him lots of love and a sense of security. Once he learns that he is loved, that he is valuable, that he is a member of the family, he can turn to others and say, "I am a person of value." His personality will develop with experience, and while his handicap will in part shape that personality, it will not define it. However, physical self-awareness is also a vital part of self-concept, and blind children need special help in developing a realistic mental image of their bodies and what they can and cannot do.

Since a blind child receives limited information about his body you need to make the most of all teaching situations. He must be given opportunities to learn about himself through real experiences, and not only by being told, "This is your hand or foot." He must feel his foot, wiggle it, learn that it belongs to him and that other people have feet too!

This chapter includes activities to help your child learn about "self" in relation to himself and to other people and objects. How you measure the success of each activity will depend on your child and you. One factor is how you look at your child's handicap and what effect your feelings have on how he looks at it. There is no line that says "success is achieved by," because you know your child best and are the best judge of what he has learned.

Suggested Activities for
the First Year

Objective: To help the blind child learn about space.
Procedure: Gently hold either the baby's wrist or ankle between the thumb and first finger and move his limbs in and out, in a circle. Repeat frequently and daily.

Objective: To help the child learn about his environment.
Procedure: Gently stroke each of his hands and feet with a towel. This should be done while the baby is lying flat on his back. Put your one arm flat on the surface behind his head. This will let him know that you are close to him. Do this exercise at least three times each day.

3 to 6 months

Objective: To draw attention to his hands.
Procedure: Play patty cake with him.
Have him help in holding his bottle.
Put mittens on his hands.
Put honey or jelly on his fingers.
All of these will force him to take note of his hands.

Objective: To learn about his mother's and father's bodies.
Procedure: Let him explore your body, by placing him across your chest as you are sitting and also when you are lying flat. Move his hands and feet around and gently talk to him.

Observation: Your child needs to be bounced and cuddled, tossed and hugged by parents, relatives and friends. An infant who lacks this stimulation often withdraws and then objects strongly to changes in lifestyle. Spend more time than usual cuddling, holding, touching, stroking and moving the baby. At the same time, talk to your baby in soothing, comforting tones. This body play is one way of telling your child how much you care for and love him; make it a meaningful and loving experience.

6 to 9 months

Objective: To encourage your baby to move his body.

Procedure: Place your child on a pad made from different materials sewn together such as pieces of a sheet or blanket to which you attach rattles, bells, or textured materials (like silk or velvet). Place your child on it and let him explore the different things that you have sewn on the pad. Place a rattle under his body to see if this will annoy him enough to make him roll over.

8 to 12 months

Objective: To learn about the parts of his body.

Procedure: During his bath, name the parts of his body as you touch them, and talk about how they move.

Encourage him to help in dressing. As you dress him, ask him to "put your arm in the sleeve" or "put your foot in the shoe."

During play, roll a ball with a bell and have him kick with his foot, punch with his fist, and slap with his open palm.

Objective: To encourage your child to explore how his own body moves.

Procedure: Place a textured pad in the bottom of the playpen. A textured pad can be made from old materials that are sewed together with toys attached to it. Attach it to the sides of the playpen with elastic rattles and keys. Place some cereal boxes and pillows on the bottom of the playpen. These objects will take up some room and this will force your baby to have to maneuver around them. Set at the side of the playpen and call him to come towards your voice. Move your position. Try this activity every day.

12 to 24 months

Objective: To encourage him to move toward an object.

Procedure: Place him on the floor or rug, turn a radio on in an opposite corner and encourage him to crawl towards the sound by using your voice. If he makes no effort to move, place your body in a crawling position over him and move his hands and feet as if he were crawling. Be sure that you move the right hand and the left foot at the same time, and then the left hand and right foot together.

Objective: To learn the parts of his body.

Procedure: Play games such as Simple Simon Says, or Head and Shoulders, Knees and Toes. As you say each part of the body, have your child place a hand on it.

24 to 36 months

Objective: To help your child to learn the functions of the parts of his body.

Procedure: During feeding and play time, talk with your child about what he is doing. For example, his hand "holds" the spoon, his foot "kicks" the ball, his teeth "chew" the food, etc.

Note: To help your baby develop a healthy, positive self-concept it is important that he have freedom of movement. Encourage him to bend, twist, stretch and swing.

The following is a suggested list of words to try to teach your child. These are body parts that your child should be able to say, point to, and know what they are able to do.

head	hair	palm
ear	neck	hip
nose	shoulders	leg
mouth	chest	knee
eyes	stomach	foot
teeth	back	ankle
tongue	arm	heel
face	hand	toes

As the baby develops language, teach him to imitate what you are saying. Use sentences like, "Tommy, this car is yours." Have him repeat the phrase and change the "yours" to "mine." At feeding time, use the phrase, "I want more," then pour a little into your glass. Have him say it and pour some into his glass. This will start him using the pronoun "I" when he wants to talk about himself. This is a difficult task — be patient and try to give him a lot of occasions to use "I," "you" and "me."

A positive self-concept is important to your child's development. Many things will contribute to how he feels about himself: being able to do things for himself, being successful in doing his jobs, being accepted and loved by those around him. If you, the important people in your child's life, treat him as though he is incapable of doing things because of his handicap, he will begin to believe it, lose interest in trying, and look upon himself as a failure. If you do things for your child because you can do them faster, he will never have the experience of doing things for himself, thus making it difficult for him to become independent. How you treat him today will be the way he will act tomorrow.

Chapter 3

Learning How to Move Around

From the moment that you realize your child is blind and cannot learn by seeing, you can begin to teach him one of the most important preschool tools—orientation. Orienting him simply means that you are going to teach him about his own body and its relationship to other people and objects. For example, the baby is *in* the crib or the baby is lying on the floor *next to* his daddy.

The child will be developing all his senses at the same time. Keeping this in mind, you have to remember to talk about your actions. It may feel strange at first to act this way but your baby will respond and it will help him to become familiar with your voice. The eye contact between mother and baby is an attachment that is hard to compensate for, but with time and practice your child will look up at you and smile when you walk into the room and say hello, indicating that he is aware of you as separate from himself.

When you place a bottle into your infant's mouth, tell him what is happening to him. Talking with your baby slowly, quietly and in short simple words can have a very soothing effect. This tends to reduce his fear and also helps him to begin to understand what you are doing when you feed him a bottle. No matter what you are doing with your child, remember to make him feel loved and secure as you hold him and speak to him.

This chapter contains exercises and activities that will help you to teach your baby about his body and how it moves. In addition to suggestions for helping you to teach him to explore the world around him, there is a section on how to protect your child by using simple safety rules around the house.

Motor Exercises

Time should be set aside each day to do motor activities with your child. A fixed, daily routine is especially important for a blind child because it eliminates uncertainty and provides a sense of security. It helps him to know what to expect and when to expect it. Start a schedule early and stick to it as much as posssible. If changes are necessary explain them to your child before they happen.

Plan several short exercise periods of five to ten minutes each day. Plan them when you are free to devote all your attention to your child, such as before giving him a bath or at bedtime. A special place is not necessary; the rug or floor makes a good exercise spot. Dress the child so he will be comfortable and able to move freely. If the child wears long pants, make sure that the crotch is pulled up to allow him free leg movement. Shoes should be taken off.

Begin with a few movements and gradually add to them as he shows more ability. Talk to your child as you put him through the movements and make the whole thing fun. The child should see these exercises as play.

The purpose of these exercises is to develop your child's natural ability to get around and to help him to have some understanding of the places he is beginning to explore. Each exercise will help your baby to grow and strengthen his body so that he will be able to orient himself in any direction. He will learn to bend, twist, stretch and reach. Remember that much time and practice will be necessary, and that "success" will not be evident immediately. To check yourself and make sure that what you are doing is working you might use a checklist. The following is an example that can be used for the motor exercises; or you can devise one of your own (Hart, 1976).

The child	child put through movement	child helps	child alone
1. Head roll			
2. Head lift			
3. Head lift and front roll			
4. Bilateral arms			
5. Bilateral legs			
6. Bilateral arms and legs			

Exercises

Objective: To teach the baby to roll his head.

Procedure: Place the child on his back, lying on his bed or on the floor, with his legs out straight and his hands at his side. Kneel above his head and place your hands on the sides of his head. Gently turn his head from side to side, touching each ear to the bed or floor. Do not move his shoulders or the rest of his body. Talk to your baby to let him know what you are doing. You can say, "turn left, turn right," in a rhythmic tone. Always praise him by saying "good boy" or some other approving phrase. Once he starts to help you, note it on your checklist. Help until he is able to move his head alone.

Objective: To teach the baby to lift his head.

Procedure: Begin by having the child lie face down with his legs out straight. Place one of your hands under his chin and the other hand on the back of his head. Gently lift his head off the floor. His shoulders and chest should remain on the floor with only his head moving. As he learns to move his head help him less and less.

Objective: To teach him how to do a head lift and front roll.

Procedure: Combine the first two exercises. Place your hands on the side of his head. Touch his chin to his chest as you do the head roll exercise. Once you see that he no longer needs your help, let him do it by himself.

Bilateral Movements

A young child learns to move both arms and legs together before he learns to move them separately. Therefore, he should do exercises involving both before he attempts to do them alone or in an alternating action. Remember to talk to your child as you exercise. Spend only a short amount of time at each exercise session with your child. You do not want him to become bored or tired.

Place the child on his back. His legs should be straight out with his legs relaxed and knees straight but not stiff. Kneel above the child and move him through the following positions:

- Raise his arms with his elbows straight from his sides to touch his ears. Then move them back to his sides. Move his legs apart as far as they will go and then move them back together again.
- Grab the ankles and wrist on one side of his body. Move his leg as far out as it will go and at the same time move the child's arm so that it touches his ear. Do the movements at the same time. As soon as he shows that he can do it by himself, withdraw your help.

Before your child learns to creep or walk he must learn to move his arms and legs alternately so that he will be able to maintain his balance. Kneeling beside your child, put him through the following movements:

- The child should be lying on his back. With his elbows straight, move his arm until it touches his ear. Return it to his side. Do the same with his other arm. Continue the exercise, alternating the arms.
- With the legs straight, spread one as far as it will go. Return it to its position. Do the same with the other leg. Alternate the legs.

After the child is able to alternate arm and leg movements by himself, he will then be ready to do simple body exercises using his arms and legs.

Body Image

As your baby passes from infancy into the toddler years, he will want to know more about what he looks like and what other people look like. The tactual sense or sense of touch will play a major role in your child's learning. He will learn to "see" largely through touching. As you teach your child about body image, remember to describe to him what it is he is touching so that he will begin to associate the way something feels with what it is. The following list will be a guide to the body parts that he should recognize so that he will be able to get a "picture" of himself.

face	eyes	ears	mouth
chin	neck	chest	shoulders
hips	back	arm	stomach
hand	elbow	wrist	fingers
legs	ankle	knee	heel
feet	toes		

Once the child has learned the body parts, talk about them in relation to specific objects in his environment:

head to table	mouth to spoon	shoulder to wall
hands to door	back to wall	fingers to book
elbows to table	nose to book	chest to bed
knees to floor	ear to towel	wrist to chair
ankles to floor		stomach to table

Each of these situations can be acted out by you and your child. As you say them have him put himself in the correct position. An example would be when you say head to table, he should put his head down flat on the table. You can actually play a game with this activity.

It is also fun to name a part of the body and then have him do something with that part. An example of this "action game" is when you say "hands" he would then *clap* his hands. If you said "knees" he would *bend* his knees. If you said "toes" he would *wiggle* his toes. This can be played the other way. You say an action word and he has to name a part of the body and act out what it means. For example, when you say "mouth" he would say "open" and then show you an open mouth. Or when you say "feet" he would say "march," and then get up and show you what it means to march.

Once he has an idea of what he looks like, talk about the function of the different body parts. You can play a game. For every correct answer give him much praise. You may want to set a specific reward like an ice cream cone if he does well. Have him complete the phrase and point to the correct part of the body.

I see with my _____.
I hear with my _____.
I smell with my _____.
I chew with my _____.
I bite with my _____.
I talk with my _____.
I clap with my _____.
I walk with my _____.
I jump with my _____.
I run with my _____.

The blind child will also need help to understand the "picture" of another person. He should be allowed to explore another person's body by using his hands—touching, feeling, comparing and shaping. Encourage him to ask questions. The child should be helped to describe himself and others. Be sure that the person he is going to touch is comfortable with the idea and will not react negatively or awkwardly.

Travel

Once your child is walking encourage him to explore. Help him to locate objects he can walk around. Furniture, especially tables and the fronts of couches, are good objects for your child to hold on to as he walks. While a child is using the furniture and walls for support, he is also making a mental map of where things are. And because a map is no good without the names of places on it, give the objects your child touches names. This is daddy's chair, this is your rocking chair, this is the hall to your room. You are giving him the basics for independent travel. Never leave your child alone in open space. Always place him in contact with something, even a wall or a table. If your child is going to be using a room often take him around it a few times and show him where things are kept. This will help him when he is by himself.

Words
to Know

Once your child is able to talk you will be teaching him concepts. To help him travel alone, it is important that he learns the meaning of certain directional words and phrases. You will be able to tell if he really understands them if he can put them into practice. For example, "left" and "right" are two very important concepts. To tell whether he has learned them, ask him while he is seated at a table to pick up a toy on the left side of his chair and put it down on the right of the chair. He should be able to do this without a mistake once he has learned the meaning of the words.

The visually handicapped child needs to learn the relationship between his body parts and the objects around him. He will need to understand their respective meanings so that he will be able to act them out. Therefore, it is important that you help your son or daughter to understand the following words and to demonstrate that understanding.

left	level	circle	pointed
right	slant	square	blunt
incline/decline	next to	rectangle	sharp
bottom	opposite	oval	dull
far/near	curved	triangle	jagged
over/under	further		
above/below	around	yard	round
forward/backward	sideways	foot	arc
inside/outside	distance	inches	middle
up/down	away from	mile	diagonal
narrow/wide	straight		parallel
short/long	crooked	second	perpendicular
big/small	bent	minute	
rough/smooth	overhang	hour	gutter
high/low	in front of		curb
soft/hard	size		sidewalk
thick/thin	S—curve		

Making Comparisons

To help your child form a picture of an object, compare things according to their weight, size, shape, thickness and temperature. Play guessing games about objects. For example, play "which is bigger" using the furniture. Let him experience how different surfaces feel. Together, get on your knees and crawl around on the floor, the rug, the grass, the sidewalk, and other surfaces you can think of, and describe these various experiences explaining that the grass is damp, the snow is wet, and the floor is hard.

Walking Indoors

The blind child will easily adapt to changes in flooring from carpet to tile or to rugs. This can best be done if he walks barefoot in the beginning. Have him tell you about what he is feeling under his feet. Have him put his shoes on and ask him to tell you about the feel of the floor and discuss the difference.

Stairs

Learning how to go up steps is easier than learning how to come down. The toddler holding onto the rail with one hand can be taught to climb the steps by placing both feet on each step. As he gets older, he will learn to put only one foot on a step at a time.

Objective: To learn how to climb stairs.
Procedure: Have your child grasp the handrail with one hand. Do not let him use two hands and pull himself up the steps. Keep his body facing straight ahead rather than towards the handrail.

Have him place one foot on the first step. Then bring the second foot up to the first step. Repeat this procedure until he gets to the top of the staircase. Do not let him stop in the middle. He must learn from the beginning that you climb all the way to the top or the bottom. If he forgets where he is he could step off into mid-air and fall.

To teach him to go down use the same procedure. Let him hold the rail with one hand and step down, again placing two feet on each step.

Note: Remember that stairways are hazardous for blind children. Use gates to protect your child until he is old enough to understand how to use stairs safely. A small piece of carpet can also be nailed at the top and bottom of the staircase as a landmark. When the toddler gets older and becomes more familiar with the stairs he will learn to place only one foot on each step. Climbing stairs takes time and practice. Encourage your child to climb by counting the steps and praising him for his effort.

Walking Outdoors

Learning to walk outdoors can be a little scary at first. The blind child expects all floors to be made out of tile or carpet or wood. As one little boy said: "The grass is sharp and prickly; the gravel is wobbly and slips under my feet, and sidewalks have edges for falling off." Take your child on a nature walk. Describe what surrounds him. Let him explore as much of the environment as possible. If you have an enclosed yard, take your child around and show him a few landmarks. Maybe an old apple tree or swing set will be enough to let him set up his own "map" of the yard. Do not put his toys in the middle of the yard; place them near one of the landmarks so that he can locate them by himself.

Safety Precautions

In order to make your home a little safer for a blind child you may want to take steps to safeguard your child from:

- sharp edges by cutting tennis balls in half and attaching them to the corners of tables and other furniture.
- gas flames by shutting the pilot light off and using matches when you want to light your stove.
- windows by keeping them locked. If they must be opened, open them from the top. Do not trust a screen to support your child's weight.
- appliances with cords by putting the appliance away when you are finished with it. If the cord must stay out, tape it on to the floor.
- electric sockets by getting safety caps and putting them on any plug that is not in use.
- staircases by putting a gate up.
- doors by insisting that all doors be either kept open all the way or closed all the way. It is very dangerous to leave them ajar.

Reference

Hart, V. *Beginning with the handicapped.* Springfield, Ill.: Charles C Thomas, 1978.

Chapter 4

Playing and
Learning

When children are playing, they are also learning. Although parents play with their children from time to time and are available to provide assistance and settle arguments, they mostly give their children the playthings and let them play by themselves. With your blind child the balance of assistance will be somewhat different. You will need to take a more active role in his learning how to play. Since toys that are visually interesting will not attract him, you will need to provide him with toys that appeal to him through his other senses — toys with different textures, shapes, and noises. However, you cannot depend on the toy to attract and hold his attention because he may not know how to use it. The story of Jimmy and his new dump truck serves as an example.

Jimmy received a new dump truck from his father for his birthday. He picked the truck up and hit the wheels with his hand. For the next three days the only thing Jimmy did with his new truck was to spin the wheels. His father wondered why he didn't take it out to his sandbox and play with it there. What Jimmy's father did not realize was that Jimmy, who is blind, had no way of knowing what he could do with his new truck. Toys and some of the ways they can be used need to be described to blind children. Then they can play with them and discover by themselves other ways of enjoying them.

There is no need for special toys for children with little or no sight. The appeal of the toy is not in looking at it but in what the child can do with it. Blind children prefer toys that they can use actively. Toys that have an interesting feel, taste or smell can often be found around the house. Examples are: nesting cups which are made from four different size cans; jars and bottles with lids that can be used for matching, screwing , unscrewing, pouring and filling; and old fashioned nuts and bolts from a hardware store.

The following are some toy suggestions for different age groups.

For
Infants

Rattles of many different types: weighted, tinkly, wobbly rattles, suction rattles, homemade rattles that are crocheted or sewn with a bell inside, tin or plastic containers with bells, dry macaroni or beans inside; it is important that the rattles be easy for the baby to hold.

Cuddly or furry toys do not have the same appeal to blind children that they do for sighted youngsters. You may want to attach a bell to a cuddly toy to make it more appealing.

Water toys which stick to the side of the tub and toys for pouring and floating help to make bathtime an interesting and fun time.

Musical toys such as wind chimes, tone bells and music boxes are good, but only if used occasionally and for a short time. Constant use becomes noise to the infant instead of stimulation or enjoyment.

Mobiles are especially useful for the blind infant. They can be homemade from coat hangers, nylon thread and objects that make sounds. Hang the objects on the hanger low enough so that the infant can hit it with random movements from his hands while in the crib.

A crib gym can be made by tying a cord across the crib or baby carriage and attaching plastic bracelets, bells, rattles and spoons to it. Homemade balls and a commercially made busy box can be enjoyed by the blind child when he is in his crib or playing on the floor.

As the child gets older his interests will change and other types of toys will bring him more enjoyment.

For Toddlers and Preschoolers

Educational toys that help your child to learn size, shape and number concepts are especially appropriate for this age group. Examples of these are stacking toys, nesting toys and shape puzzles with large pieces.

Push-pull toys are a lot of fun. Doll carriages, wagons with high handles and little shopping carts help your child to learn how to walk because the child can put his weight on these as he pushes them around.

Friction cars are interesting because your child can follow where they are going by listening to the noise. Such toys are good because they accustom him to following sound cues.

Band instruments are loved by all—except possibly parents. A tin can makes a lovely drum; a wooden spoon to hit the drum with and you are all ready to play band! Harmonica, tambourine and drums are the easiest for your child to handle.

Blocks which interlock are particularly good for your child. Try to use a set that is large because his fingers may not be able to work the small block sets. Peg boards and stringing beads or buttons can help to improve the child's ability to use toys that require the use of fingers rather than hands.

Dolls are a great source of fun and learning. Your child—boy or girl—will enjoy playing with them, and will learn about body parts and dressing, among other things.

Make a "what is it?" box and put all different objects into it and let your child pull them out and tell you all about them. Try to use items that are familiar to him until he gets used to playing the game. Praise him for his answers.

When your child is ready to use crayons you can make it more interesting by placing a piece of window screening or wire gauze under the page to be colored. Then when the child is finished drawing and the screen is removed, he will be able to feel where he has drawn because the texture of the paper will be different.

To teach tracing to your child, take a piece of heavy duty paper and place it on top of an open phone book. Then take a tracing wheel from a sewing kit and show your child how to follow the edges of whatever shape you are tracing. Wooden shapes are easier to use because they can be held in place as you trace around them and you don't have to worry about cutting them. When you are finished turn the page over and your child will be able to feel a raised outline of the shape. These shapes can then be cut out with blunt-nosed scissors.

Play dough, clay, finger paints and brush painting are all activities that your child should have fun doing. Help him to make things and then give them away as presents. This will give him a great sense of accomplishment and will promote social development.

Many activities can be centered around the use of play dough. A simple, inexpensive recipe for homemade play dough follows:

    2 cups of flour
    1 cup of salt
    2 tablespoons of olive oil.

Knead together the flour, the salt and the oil and you have play dough! This will keep for weeks if kept in a plastic bag or in a jar in the refrigerator.

Roller skates and tricycles are a great source of bangs and bruises but are of tremendous enjoyment to the blind child who, like his sighted peers, enjoys the sensation of his body in motion. Encourage your child to try these.

Toy phones and tape recorders are learning toys for the blind child. Play games with your child as you teach him how to use both items. They will become a necessary part of his life and should be introduced in a light enjoyable way.

Rainy Day Activities (Taylor, 1974)

Here are some rainy day activities which the blind child can enjoy:

1. Put clothespins on the side of a shoe box.
2. Pull clothespins off the side of the box and place them in the box.
3. Scrub wall, table, floor with wet rag.
4. Sit on the floor with legs apart and roll a ball back and forth with a partner.
5. Screw tops off small jars to find a reward inside.
6. Put screw tops back on the small jars.
7. Using a dish pan or baby bath learn to fill and empty small cups.
8. Climb up on a small box and jump off.
9. Play inside a large carton making it fall over and then righting it.
10. Fit several different size cans inside one another.
11. Hammer several large nails into a piece of soft wood. This should be done with supervision until the child can do it without hammering his fingers.
12. Put spools on a long spindle.
13. String large beads on a shoe lace.
14. Clap in rhythm to the music coming from a record or radio.

Toy Safety

When buying a toy for a child with limited vision it is important to choose one that does not have any sharp points. Since young children often put toys in their mouths, it should not have small removable parts that could be swallowed. Be sure that the paint or coloring on the toy is non-toxic. Outdoors, alert your child to toys that may be in motion such as a swing, teeter-totter, or merry-go-round.

Rhythm and Finger Play

As your child grows he will enjoy songs and nursery rhymes. Some that have been found to be most enjoyed by children are: pat-a-cake, this little pig, one, two, buckle my shoe and row, row, row your boat.

A sense of rhythm is important for your child to develop. Frequently take him in your arms and dance around the room with him to the rhythm of music. This will help him to get a sense of how your body moves to music and it will give him an idea of how his should move.

Playmates

Playmates are a must for your child! Encourage your neighbors'or relatives' children to visit and play with your child. Give a very simple explanation about your child being blind.

Children accept parents' explanations without many questions. Be prepared that when there are other children around there will be the usual amount of spats and near disasters. Try to stay out of the squabbles and let the children handle them on their own. They will not give any special attention to your child. They will treat him like the rest of their friends, which is the way you will want it. Try not to be overprotective or what happened to Mrs. Tupper could happen to you.

Paul had his two friends, Mat and Jack, over to play. They were outside playing on the teeter-totter and having lots of fun. All of a sudden, Mrs. Tupper looked out the window and saw that the boys would not let her son on the teeter-totter. She came flying out the back door, yelling at Matt and Jack. They were scared and did not understand what they had done to deserve such a scolding. Crying, they left the yard as Mrs. Tupper yelled, "Don't come back until you're ready to behave and not be mean." They did not come back all that week or the next. Mrs. Tupper watched Paul roam around the house looking sad. He missed his friends. Mrs. Tupper realized she had overreacted. It took another week to coax the children to come back. She was sorry and told them about it. The one that had suffered was Paul because he had missed playing with his two friends.

Outdoors offers an opportunity for noisy and active play. It gives your child the experience of a large space with fewer physical restrictions. The outdoors is also better for encouraging other children to come over and play. The equipment that you use should have no sharp points. A slide, jungle gym and sandbox are all good choices for backyard or playground activities. Be aware that your child will need to know the boundaries.

As your child gets older, you can introduce him to sports, hobbies and other pastimes. Pets are great fun. They are stimulating, active and lovable. Playing with them will help your child to use many of his senses. In addition, helping to take care of a pet teaches your child a sense of responsibility.

Encourage your child to participate actively in sports that are geared to his age. Swimming, roller skating, ice skating and skiing are some of the activities that blind or visually impaired children enjoy. Bowling has been adapted through special equipment (a portable guide rail) so that your child can participate. Some ball games can be played with sound-producing balls. Jogging, running, and bike riding can be enjoyed by all members in a family. Until your child can ride a bike, you may want to attach a seat to the back of your bike to familiarize him with the sensation. He can then be gradually introduced to a tandem or two-seated bike.

When you are playing with your child, remember the main purpose is to have fun; so relax and enjoy it.

Reference

Taylor, B. *Blind preschool: A manual for parents of blind preschool children.* Colorado Springs: Industrial Printers of Colorado, 1974.

Chapter 5

Daily Living Skills

Most children at an early age watch parents, brothers, and sisters clean their teeth, brush their hair and wash their hands, and try to copy them. Blind children cannot imitate you in the same manner. You will need to describe to your child the actions involved and physically guide him through them.

Do not be afraid to start teaching daily living skills as early as possible. He needs to learn them in a loving manner. He needs you—your understanding, humor and patience—to encourage him to want to learn. He needs to discover that he can do things for himself; to know that although he is blind, he is more the "same as" than he is "different from." It is important that you give simple directions. Be consistent and firm. Blind children, like all children, need discipline. Do not use a separate set of rules for him and another for his sister or brother. Try not to let pity enter into your expectations. Set up realistic goals and explain to him what you are teaching him and why. Make a checklist and praise him each step of the way for good performance. Do not settle for second best if you know that he can do better. Neighbors, friends and relatives can help, but you as his parents must set the example. Tender loving care and an insistence on your part that he practice and learn will help him to become an independent and accepted member of the sighted world in which he lives.

Independence

The desire for independence and social acceptance will be expressed at some point in your child's life. You can help him to prepare for it by giving him a secure home from which he can explore his environment and meet new people; also, the knowledge that you have *accepted* his blindness and that together you are going to learn how to live with it. Acceptance is a must before he can develop into a loving and responsive child. Let your child know that you love him and are proud of him as he is. This will let him see himself as worthwhile to himself and others. It will also help him to want to do things for himself as well as for others.

Remember to be patient and choose simple things at the beginning. At first, the tasks may seem overwhelming but when they are done as part of the every day normal routine they will not be too much. You have to remember, too, that you have needs of your own. Plan a shopping trip without the children or a luncheon date with your husband or a friend. Don't forget everyone else and devote all your time to your blind child. You would be punishing yourself if you did. Also, you would be denying your child the experiences of meeting other people.

This chapter is divided into four sections: (1) feeding, which includes drinking and eating; (2) personal care, which includes the use of the bathroom and taking care of one's body; (3) behavior which is socially unacceptable; and (4) dressing, which includes both taking clothes off and putting them on.

Feeding

Feeding suggestions start with drinking because this is the natural starting point for all infants. Sucking on a nipple gives pleasure as well as strength to the muscles that will be used later for chewing. Following are ideas that may be helpful or which may answer some of the questions you have.

Drinking

While your baby is using the bottle, encourage him to put both hands on it so that he will eventually learn to support it by himself.

Introduce the change from breast feeding or bottle feeding to using a cup in the same way and at the same stage as you would with a sighted child, usually at about twelve months. If your baby rejects the cup at the beginning, wait a few days and try again.

Observations

Questions often come to mind from friends and neighbors, as is seen in this conversation between Mrs. Brown and Mrs. Monday:

Mrs. Brown was having coffee with her friend Mrs. Monday, a mother of a four-year-old blind girl. "Why do blind children frequently drop their glass after taking a drink?" asked Mrs. Brown. Without hesitating, Mrs. Monday answered, "Because the glass is given to them out of mid-air and so they return it to the same invisible shelf!"

What Mrs. Monday was trying to tell Mrs. Brown was that blind children need a reference point. They cannot follow the action with their eyes so they need a starting point and a finishing point. Place the glass on the table (the reference point) and let the blind child pick it up from there. When he goes to put it down he will put it back in the same spot. Also, when you are getting a drink for a young blind child, do not fill it more than half way. This helps him to drink it without spilling it.

Pouring

When you are ready to teach your child how to pour a glass of milk or water for himself be prepared for a few spills. Have a washcloth handy. And let him learn how to wipe up spills at the same time as you are teaching him how to pour. With a fair amount of water in a pitcher, have your child put his finger over the edge of a glass, then slowly pour the water into the glass and stop when he says he can feel it. Repeat this a few times until you are sure he is feeling the water as it touches his finger and he is not guessing based on the sound of the water going into the glass. Next, place his hand on the handle of the pitcher and pour the water together. Have him say, "Stop," when he can feel it touch his fingertips. Use a lightweight pitcher and a sturdy glass so that he will be able to try it by himself. As you go through the motions a few times ask him to describe what is happening so that you are sure that he understands. Then let him try it on his own. To encourage him, have him fill the juice glasses in the morning or pour the milk with lunch. Praise him for his efforts.

Eating

Visually impaired toddlers are often poor eaters. Since they are unaware of the variety of meals the family enjoys, they are often unwilling to try new foods. The introduction of different flavors and textures during the first year of life will encourage them to eat more of a variety later on. For example, a teaspoon of boiled rice added to pureed vegetables will give a different texture and get the tongue used to handling small lumps.

Have other members of the family tell him what a new food is called and what it tastes like. Try to use highly descriptive and distinctive words in describing different tastes, e.g., *sour* for pickles; *sweet* for icing on a cake; *cold* for lettuce; *hot* for soup. (Recognize that soup is hard to eat unless it is full of crackers and bread.) Remember that a blind child depends largely on his sense of touch, and it will probably take a little convincing before he will hold something that is unpleasant to the touch, such as a cold, wet piece of orange or apple.

Finger feeding

Finger feeding should be introduced just as soon as the baby has learned to put his hand to his mouth. Foods that have strong smells and flavors seem to be better accepted for sucking and licking by the child who cannot see. Examples of these foods are soft bacon, ginger snaps, a piece of garlic sausage and celery sticks. He will not be able to bite off pieces but they are much more interesting than the usual teething biscuits.

Spoon feeding

Finger feeding of small, bite-sized pieces of vegetables, non-greasy bacon and crackers should be started before attempting to teach the use of a spoon. Permit touching of unfamiliar food, but not playing with it. When you are spoon feeding your child, use two spoons. Let him hold one while you feed him with the other. Encourage your child to try to feed himself with a spoon. Be prepared for a mess; all children make one when they are learning to feed themselves. Put a bib on him and keep a washcloth handy. In the beginning, use food that will stay on the spoon easily, like mashed potatoes. Be sure that the pieces of food are small enough for your child to handle easily. Stand behind him when showing him how to use a spoon. Sing a song as you do it: dip, slide and into your mouth or dip, push and lift to your mouth. Whatever choice of words you make, repeat them each time until he can do it without hearing the words. Once he gets the motion of the spoon being lifted to his mouth, you can guide him by using his elbow.

Introduce a fork after he has fully learned how to use a spoon. Again, stand behind him when you are teaching him how to use a fork. Try to start with food that does not slide off the fork, like turnips or mashed potatoes. Show him how the fork can be tilted and used to spear food like a piece of meat, or how it can be used to lift food into the mouth. It will take practice before he will learn how to get food on his fork each time.

Give him as much verbal direction as he needs in the beginning. You want him to learn, not to become frustrated. Once he has mastered the fork and spoon then explain what the knife does. When you think he is ready to learn how to use a knife, repeat the procedure used above. Standing behind him, move his hands with yours in a cutting motion. Do this often and explain what it is you are doing and how the blade cuts the meat. Have him try it alone, watching to make sure that he doesn't cut himself.

The American Foundation for the Blind publishes a book which describes various home utensils that are made especially for the blind. A knife with a safety blade which prevents the user from cutting himself when it is used properly is one of these special utensils.

Self-feeding

The child's playing with food becomes a problem only if the parents react to it. Rather than create a problem, help your child to develop good eating habits. Allow the first few minutes to be a time when he feeds himself. Praise him for a job well done. If you see him starting to lose interest, talk to him and encourage him to keep eating. If this does not work, feed him. Remember it is important for toddlers to get the proper nourishment. Dinner should be a time which is pleasant for everyone; a time when the family is together and can talk to one another. It should not become a chore or a battle to get your child to feed himself. As he grows older he will not want to be spoon-fed and will then assume more of the responsibility for feeding himself.

Table setting

Always set the table the same way. Forks on the left, spoon and knife on the right, glass at the top of the knife. The first few times you teach him about his plate and what is around it, be sure you stand behind him so that you will be able to take his hand and let him touch each utensil as it is mentioned. When you put the food on his plate, tell him where it is, e.g., meat at the bottom, potatoes on the left, vegetables at the top. Or, if he knows the clock: meat at six, potatoes at ten, and vegetables at two. When you go out to eat, quietly explain where the food is located on his plate.

Eating habits

Appetite and eating habits need not be affected by blindness, but sometimes are. Parents and others may give in to the child's whims with regard to food because he is blind. They may also expect slower progress from the bottle feeding stage to eating solid food. For blind children, gradually make the change from baby foods to junior foods to regular table foods at the same time as you would with any child. Check any eating problems with a doctor to make sure that there are no medical reasons for his not eating or chewing properly.

If chewing is delayed, first be sure that he knows what it means to chew. Let him feel your jaws as you chew on an apple and then let him feel his own jaws as you move them up and down with your hands. Also, give him crisp foods that cannot be swallowed whole, such as thin potato chips, crackers, and celery and encourage him to chew them. It must be remembered that the visual appeal of food is lacking, and you may have to talk to him while he is eating and help him to develop an interest in food. As he gets older, let him help around the kitchen, especially with making dinner. Manners can be taught as the child grows. A simple "please" and "thank you" become natural when done as part of the daily routine. Sitting straight up without slouching is a must. To avoid spilling foods, have him lean forward a little so that his mouth is over the plate. Insist that the visually impaired child act in a socially acceptable manner at the table. Such behavior, particularly as he gets older, will be important to his acceptance by sighted peers.

Personal
Care

As early as possible you should try to start a bathroom routine. For the toddler, you may want to start with teaching how to brush his teeth or comb his hair. The first step in any bathroom routine is to show your child those things that are located in the bathroom and their purposes.

Guide your child to touch each item. Let him feel the soap when it is wet and slippery as well as when it is dry. To avoid the risk of scalding, teach him to *always turn on the cold water tap first,* then the hot. Show him how to put the soap between his hands and make lather. Then rinse and dry his hands.

Place a footstool in front of the sink so he can back into it without your having to lift him. Let him explore in and around the sink. Show him how to turn the faucets on and off. Have him feel the different temperatures of the water coming out. Be sure, of course, that he doesn't burn himself. If your sink has a stopper, let the water fill up. Tell your child what is going to happen and then pull the stopper to let the water out. Since he may be afraid that he, too, will go down the drain, place a familiar small toy or doll in the sink over the drain so that he will understand that only the water will go down, leaving the toy or doll where you put it. Let him pull the plug and listen to the water going down.

Let him feel the washcloth, towels, toothbrush, comb and brush, etc. He is ready to learn routines when he shows interest and is able to follow instructions or demonstrations. Keep everything in the same place so on each additional trip to the bathroom he will become familiar with where things belong. Low hooks or towel bars will make it easier for your child to reach these items without any help. As a safety precaution, keep your bathroom door fully open or fully closed so that the child will not have to worry about walking into the door.

Stand behind your child when you are teaching him how to use a washcloth, towel, toothbrush and comb and brush. It is easier to guide his hand from this position. It may be easier for you if you sit while showing him since your body in this position will be closer to his.

Cleaning
Teeth

Use a pleasant tasting toothpaste. Stand behind the child and as he puts the toothbrush near his mouth guide it into his mouth. Then gently take his wrist and move it up and down. Repeat the whole procedure a few times. Some parents may prefer an electric toothbrush. If you do, use the techniques described earlier, but before you put the toothbrush in his mouth be sure to let him turn it on and off a couple of times. Make sure the sound of his brush does not scare him. It will be easier at the beginning if you put the toothpaste on for him; later you can teach him to do it himself. He will have to be shown how to rinse his mouth after cleaning his teeth. Let him feel your face as you rinse your mouth. Practice rinsing and describe what he is supposed to be doing as he is trying it.

Brushing
Hair

Give your child a brush or comb to play with. It doesn't really matter which one you teach first, but it is easier if you teach one at a time. Dolls' hair is usually fun to practice on. You may want to play "beauty parlor" and let him brush your hair and make believe he is giving you a new hairstyle. Then sit on a chair or on the bed and have your child stand in front of you. Put your hand over his on the comb (or brush) and go through the motion of running the comb (or brush) through his hair. Let him try to comb (or brush) your hair and the hair of other members of the family.

Bathing

Bathtime is a pleasant time to start to learn some of the skills like soaping the body or using a facecloth. Make the bath a fun experience and use bathtub toys. Use a washcloth to put the soap on his body and then show him how to wiggle his body or splash water on himself to take the soap off. Then let him put the soap on by himself. Be careful that he does not use the soap near his eyes. In much the same way you can teach him to wash his hair, but be sure to use a no-tear shampoo. When you are all finished, let him pull the plug and listen for the water to go down the drain. Tell him that this drain is like the one in the sink and only water can go down this drain. Let him feel his toys by the drain outlet and it will help him to understand that the holes are little and that he cannot possibly go through them.

Toilet
Training

Follow training procedures but realize that a longer training period may be necessary. Do not expect too much too soon. The blind or visually impaired toddler will with encouragement and patience be able to use the toilet himself.

Unacceptable
Behavior

Blind children frequently develop mannerisms such as rocking, twirling, rubbing or poking their eyes, or jumping up and down on the spot. These habits seem to develop when the blind child is bored, lonely, upset or angry. Pressing on one or both of the eyes is probably the most common habit. At about one year, your child may rub his eyes a great deal. Have them checked to make sure there is nothing medically wrong with them, but discourage your child from pressing his eyes. It is better to stop the behavior before it is too late and has become a habit. Give him a toy or other object to occupy his hands. Take him for a walk or change his position to distract him. Very few blind children suck their thumbs, and the few who do are not eye pressers, suggesting that these activities may serve the same functions for young children.

Another common behavior is rocking, which is a self-stimulating activity. Sometimes parents do not recognize this as unusual behavior in children. If you notice your child sitting in one position, not playing with anything and just rocking back and forth, gently put your hand on his shoulder and he should stop. Then give him something to do. He may be doing it because he is bored. Remember, it is harder for him to choose activities by himself because he cannot look around and find a toy which might interest him. Help to keep him busy and interested in normal activities. Other mannerisms, like jumping in one spot, may develop as a means of letting off steam. If this happens make a regular part of his day a "gym time" and let him know that this is the only time when he can do these activities which at other times are not acceptable to you. One mother used to get on a trampoline with her youngster for ten minutes each day and let him jump to his heart's content.

Other behaviors of blind children which are unacceptable are staring at lights, playing with shadows by waving their fingers in front of their eyes, nonstop loud talking, constantly rubbing their hands together, rolling their heads, and sitting or standing too close to another person. You must remember that your child is not aware of how he looks. He is depending on you to tell and show him. So it is your responsibility to kindly and lovingly point out that there are certain behaviors which are unattractive. Appeal to his sense of pride and desire to be accepted. Instead of constantly saying, "Put your hands down," which might embarrass him in front of others, try to use a secret code word that only you and your child will understand. This will take the public pressure off both of you. He can relax and know that he and you are the only two who will know what the word really means. There is a natural desire in most children to do what everyone else does, but the blind child will need extra help in learning how others behave.

The following suggestions have been found useful in reducing unacceptable mannerisms:

1. Maintain a routine of activities so that the child is not lonely or bored. Encourage other children to come over and play.

2. Check him when he is playing alone. If you see that he is doing the same thing over and over without any change (e.g., spinning the wheels of a truck), then show him another thing he can do. Set up some Cheerios that he can pick up and dump out of his truck.

3. Try not to leave your child listening to the TV or a record for too long. These passive activities may lead to your child starting a habit to stimulate himself. Let him watch TV for a short time and then ask him questions about what was on.

4. When your child is young, try not to bring attention to his actions by nagging him and saying, "Stop poking your eyes." Just gently put your hand on his shoulder to stop the rocking or simply remove the child's hand while giving him something else to do.

Note: It's much easier to stop these "blindisms" early, before they become habits. Tell him how proud you are of him when he is not doing those things which are unacceptable. It is up to you to convince him that he does not want to act in that awkward way. Enrollment in a nursery school or play school may also help the blind child to change his behavior and learn to act in socially acceptable ways, and is something you may want to consider.

Dressing

Encourage your child to become independent in dressing. As an infant, talk to him as you dress him, "Now let's put your right arm in your sleeve, now we put the left arm in, now we button up." This helps the infant to become familiar with the routine and the names of the parts of his body. By 12 months, your baby should be able to help dress himself by lifting the correct arm or leg, and by tucking his thumb under the elastic at the top of his pants and pulling up.

Simple clothing that is easy to take off and on makes dressing easier. T-shirts and other pull-overs can be laid on the bed with the back sides up and necks farthest away. This frees both hands to explore the shirt and slip it on over his head.

Safety pins or tags that the child can feel should mark the back of a garment so that he can tell it is the back. Sew these tags at the top of the inside shirt collar or at the back in the middle of the waist band on his pants.

Socks are very hard to put on because the heel always seems to end up on the wrong side. Show your child how to slide his toes in and pull the bulgy heel around under the foot. Better yet, use socks that are heel-less.

Tying shoes is best taught by the two loop method. Practicing on old shoes, use two shoe laces that have different textures to make it easier (e.g. cotton and nylon) in order for the child to distinguish between the two loops. First teach the "under" and "over" steps for making the first loop. Repeat for the second loop and then teach him to tie the two loops together to make a knot.

For a blind child, putting on his own jacket takes a lot of practice. Follow a routine and have him place one arm in first, then swing his jacket to the other side and put his other arm in. If the jacket has a zipper, use it to practice zippering. If it has buttons, teach him how to button and unbutton. Try to teach your child using real pieces of clothing rather than a tying or buttoning board.

Hats are not a favorite with blind children. They tend to interfere with their being able to use their ears to locate sounds and echoes. Tony's mother found out the hard way. Mrs. Caputo decided it was time to buy a new hat for Tony. She could not find one she liked so she knitted him one. She made him one with flaps that covered his ears, and took great pride in her accomplishment. The first time she put it on his head, he screamed to take it off. "I can't 'see' you when I wear that silly hat," he insisted. So all of her work was in vain and she had to go out and find a hat that did not cover his ears.

A child of three or four can learn to hang up a jacket on a low clothes hook and to find it there when he wants to go out. Orderly drawers and closets can make it easier for a blind child to find his clean clothes, and if you let him help you put the clothes away he will learn more readily where his socks, shirts, sweaters, etc., are kept. A shoe tree is very helpful, too.

Observation: Unfortunately dressing and undressing small children is often done at those times of the day when you are most apt to be rushed. This makes it harder to be calm and patient and try to teach your child how to dress himself. All too often if he is slow or awkward, the tendency is to give up the teaching and dress him yourself. There is no easy solution to this problem. Certainly you can do it more quickly and better, but think of all the time you will save in the future if your child learns to dress himself and how important it is for him to learn to do it for himself.

Sleeping

The sleeping patterns of totally blind children are nearly the same as their sighted peers. However, during the second year, they often reverse day and night, napping on and off during the day and sleeping only two or three hours at night. Try to discourage this by spending more time outside during the day. Let him lie awake at night unattended or you may quickly become exhausted from lack of sleep. If this continues for a long time, call your doctor and ask him for some advice. It is not unusual for blind children to require less sleep than their sighted brothers and sisters. If he wakes up early, insist that he play quietly in his crib with some of his toys. This will let the rest of the family sleep without being disturbed.

The blind child usually drops his morning nap around 12 months and the afternoon nap around his third birthday. (Any later than that is a gift to his mother.) If parents see that their child is not ready for bed until ten or eleven o'clock at night, then the nap time during the day should be shortened or ended. If the child is not sleepy when his bedtime comes, allow him to play quietly in his crib. Do not get into the habit of giving him an audience at night or he will perform all night.

Once he can climb out of his crib, night prowling could become a problem. Stop it before it starts. Use a Dutch door, if possible, and lock it. You will sleep better knowing that he cannot get out of his room and roam around the house or apartment and hurt himself. If he does get up, permit him to play quietly in his room.

These daily living skills will be learned gradually by your child. Practice them as a part of your daily routine. Encourage your child to try more on his own each day. Praise him when he tries, support him in his difficulties and love him for whatever he is able to do. And remember: never do anything for your child that he is capable of doing himself.

Chapter 6

Touch, Listen
and See

The world of the blind child is not separate from yours. It is the same. Your child will eat, play and travel in a sighted world. He will learn and grow in the same visually oriented world you do. What will be different for your child will be how he does it.

The blind child will learn to use all his senses simultaneously in order to understand the world around him. He will not only touch the music box, he will listen to hear if it makes a sound; he will feel it to see if it is hard or soft, and he will put it in his mouth to see if he can chew it. Together, these impressions will give him a "picture" of the music box so that he too can "see" it and say "how pretty it looks." The vocabulary of the blind child is the same as the sighted child's. Certain words will have more meaning to him than others. "Hot," for example, will be more readily understood than "large"; others, like colors, will have no meaning. The more experiences he has, the better developed his senses will become.

This chapter is divided into four sections, each containing some ideas about how to help your child develop his senses. Activities are given so that you will be able to teach your child in a normal, natural way as part of the daily routine.

Touching

The hands of the blind child are often called his "eyes" because the child gathers the most information about the world around him through touch. Learning by touching is limited, however, and the blind child may not get all the information he needs to form an accurate picture of an object. This is especially true in the case of large objects. Tommy, a blind three-year-old, had this problem; the following story explains.

Tommy went all over with his mother. They lived in the country so they always traveled by car. As a baby, Tommy was carried and put into his car seat. When he was a toddler he would walk to the car and climb onto the back seat and sit with his seat belt on. When he was four, his uncle asked him what he thought a car looked like. "Like a couch with wheels on it," he answered.

This story clearly shows that unknown to the people who live and play with him, he may be developing concepts that are only partly correct, or which are, in fact, completely wrong. You need to give your child an opportunity to explore his environment to help him form a complete picture. He will not be able to experience all objects in their entirety because some objects are too big, such as trees or skyscrapers. In instances like this, the child will depend on you to describe the object to him. Use words he understands. Sometimes plastic toy models can be useful. Or, you can create something that will give him more information. For example, to give him a sense of what a tunnel is, you can make one out of clay or cardboard and he can put his hand through it. When your child is touching something, help him to understand its shape and size. Start by using words like round, square, small, medium and large. Try to compare it to something he is already familiar with, maybe a toy or a piece of furniture. Ask him if it is "bigger than" or "smaller than" the toy. As he gets older, he will want to know the texture of things. Start as soon as he is able to understand words like rough and smooth. Make a textured pad by sewing different types of material together, e.g., velvet, corduroy, silk, etc., and put it in his playpen or on the floor where he plays. Remember, it is not true that the blind have a "sixth sense" or an innately superior sense of touch.

Their sense of touch becomes highly developed only with a lot of training and practice. Following are some suggestions for helping your child to learn by using his sense of touch.

Activities

1. Give an infant toys that he can touch, like bells, rattles and mobiles. Encourage him to hold his bottle himself.

2. Encourage a toddler to explore all over the house. Leave different objects on the floor to capture his attention, such as tennis balls, old leather pocketbooks, pots and lids, and flat plastic dishes.

Since young children frequently put anything and everything they can find into their mouths, be careful not to select objects that could be swallowed or that have parts which can be easily broken off. Use unbreakable objects.

3. Take your toddler outside or to a park and let him play on the grass. Talk with him about the feel of the grass, the leaves and the dirt. Take his shoes off and let him walk around with you in his bare feet. In the winter, take him out in the snow. Gradually let him feel the snow, how cold it is, how heavy it is, how it melts. Talk about these experiences with your child. Make sure he understands them.

4. Start your child eating finger foods such as carrots and celery which are cut into different shapes. Play "guess the shape" as he munches.

5. As your child gets older he will have fun with large pop-it beads, plastic shapes on a chain, rubber squeaky toys, strings of beads, wind-up musical toys, cradle gyms, vegetable brushes and measuring spoons.

6. When he enjoys sitting at a table, teach him how to use a peg board. Place the pegs in the board and then show him how to peg a circle or a square shape. Play along with him until he understands what you are doing.

7. Take empty spools of thread and cover them with different types of material. Let your child touch these and talk about what he feels. Then you can teach him how to string them together with a shoelace.

8. Empty cans covered with material are also fun to play with. Be sure that there are no rough edges. If they have lids that match, your child can have fun trying to put them back on. A great game to play is to take the can and place a jellybean or some other treat inside and put the lid on. Give the can back to your child and tell him if he opens the can he will find a surprise. You may want to ask him to guess what it is from the sound it makes when when he shakes it.

9. Many children's books have textured illustrations which you can use when your child is old enough for you to read to him.

Once your child is old enough to walk around and ask questions about how and why things feel the way they do, he is ready for "touching tours."

Touching
Tours

1. At home, make a tour of each room, one at a time. Spend more time in the bathroom and kitchen. Be patient and explain what each object is and what it does, as he touches it. In the kitchen, let him examine the appliances, food in the refrigerator, etc.

2. Supermarkets make interesting touching tours. As you do your shopping, take your child with you. Tell him why and how you pick the food you do. Describe how the food is packed: in cans, jars, boxes or plastic containers. Encourage him to use his sense of smell to

tell what fruits and vegetables you are picking. Give them to him and let him put them in the plastic bag.

3. Zoos are a great place for a touching tour. Some have sections where children can pet and learn a lot about the sizes, shapes and textures of animals by feeling them. Check with your local park or tourist department to see if there is a zoo of this type close to where you live.

4. Many high schools and colleges sponsor "petting musical instrument days" when children can play and touch all the instruments. Contact your local high school or college to see if this type of experience is available.

A house, during its various stages of construction, can be a fascinating experience for a blind child. He can get a picture of how a house is built by touching the foundation, and later the frame and interior. Often you can ride around your neighborhood and find one under construction.

Other touching tours might include an exploration of a car and all that is under the hood; a trip to a bakery to learn how breads and cakes are made; a trip to the seashore to search for crabs, lobsters and shells, to build sandcastles and play in the water; a trip to the firehouse to climb over the fire engines and to feel the equipment.

You will be able to think of other touching tours — a trip to a farm or a department store. Remember that you want to have fun with your child as he is learning by touching. Keep the child's interest and safety as your most important considerations.

Listening

Spoken language plays a very important role in the life of a blind child. This is particularly true during the first years of life when his direct experiences of the world are limited and he necessarily depends on others to tell him about the missing pieces. To a considerable extent, then, spoken language is vital to the blind child's understanding of the world, and eventually, of course, his primary means of communication. For this reason, it is important that his hearing be checked regularly.

Development of his listening sense must begin during the earliest weeks of the blind infant's life. He needs to be talked to frequently and to recognize the warmth of his parents' voices. Since sounds seem to come from nowhere and are largely indistinguishable for the sightless child, (much the way cocktail party chatter sounds to us), the sound of a familiar voice will help him to learn that different sounds have different and important meanings. While the occasional use of radio or television as a source of sound is fine, nothing can substitute for the sound of your voice as you hold and cuddle your baby.

As he grows, tell him about everyday household sounds such as doorbells, knocks on the door, radios, ringing telephones, television, electric appliances, shavers and hair dryers which are familiar to him. If possible, let him feel the sound source. If you are using a vacuum cleaner, for example, explain the purposes of the motor and the switch. Let him turn the vacuum cleaner on and off, and place his hand by the hose so that he can feel the suction.

When you are outdoors, describe the sounds of cars, trucks, sirens, birds, rain, etc. Help your child to pay attention to sounds, whether indoors or outdoors, by turning in the direction from which they are coming. Play games in which he must point, walk or turn toward the sound source, e.g., a ticking clock, a playing radio, church bells. As he gets older, he will be able to identify sound sources, a facility which is important to the development of orientation and mobility skills.

After the age of two years, the listening skills of a blind child generally improve at a faster rate. He will begin to understand and match the sounds to their source. Toy instruments are good to use—a bit noisy—but they teach him that he too can make sounds. Drums, trombone and cymbals will help him to understand that different sounds are heard when you do different things to the instruments.

An activity that is good for sharpening your child's sense of listening is playing *Sound Matching Board*, produced by the American Printing House for the Blind (see p. 39).

Objective: To teach the child to identify similar or dissimilar sounds.

Equipment: Two sets of small, covered metal film cans. Each set includes six cans, each with a different object inside it so that when it is shaken it will make a different noise. One set of cans is marked on the lids for the parents; the other set of cans is for the child.

Procedure: Place the twelve cans on the table. Let your child play with them for a few minutes. Then give your child the unmarked set and you take the marked one. Pick up one of your cans and shake it. Then ask your child to find among his, the one that makes the same noise as the one you are shaking. If the child shakes a can that makes a different sound, tell him that his can makes a different sound and shake your can again; encourage him to pick up another can. Keep this up until he finds the one that matches yours.

Continue the game until the child can match all the sound cans or until the child loses interest.

Another way of increasing your child's ability to listen is to sing songs and recite nursery rhymes together.

Objective: To increase child's ability to listen.

Activity: Singing Old MacDonald.

Procedure: Choose an animal you wish to act out. Your child picks one. If he does not pick one, give him one. Then have him "listen" for his part in the song and pretend to be that animal. He is responsible for making the noises of that animal whenever needed during the song. You also pretend to be an animal and act out your part when it is your turn. Repeat frequently until your child gets used to singing his part without having to be told.

Success is achieved when you can play the record and your child sings when he hears his part on the record.

When he gets older, you can play word sound games. Examples of these are included so that you can make up your own.

Examples: 1. Say which of the three words does not begin like the others: run, Tom, red. You would sound each one out and say that Tom does not because it starts with a 't' sound.
2. Say which pairs of words are the same. Then you would say:
>   bat - back
>   eat - beat
>   bang - bang

You would then point out that the only one that was the same was bang and bang.
3. Say whether the words are different. Then you would say:
>   sleep - slip
>   beat - beat

You would then point out that the one that was different was sleep and slip.

4. Give another word that rhymes with the word you say. You then say beat; your child should say: meat, seat, or any other word that rhymes with beat.

Your child's blindness does not mean he can't hear, so remember to keep sounds at a normal level. This includes other people; discourage them from shouting at your child.

Speaking

Children who cannot see facial expressions depend largely on a person's choice of words and tone of voice. It is easy for a child to receive the wrong message, as happens when a father, talking abruptly because he is in a hurry to get to work on time, sounds angry to the child because he cannot see him rushing around. Try to become more aware of this potential for misinterpretation and be more careful about what you say and how you say it. Remember, too, that powerful messages are sent by physical affection. A gentle hug on the way out can reassure the child that all is well. The blind child is sensitive to the moods of the people around him. He is liable to sense the anger or impatience in the hands that change him or dress him; or the quick, angry footsteps; or the strain in a familiar voice. Take care to talk about your feelings even though he is only a baby.

In order for your child to develop good speaking skills he needs experience in listening and speaking. He especially needs to hear two-way conversations: his parents talking to one another, and older children talking to their parents. Unfortunately, television has reduced the amount of time family members spend talking to each other. He also needs to participate in conversations. All too often, parents guess what their blind child wants and get it for him before he can even ask for it. This discourages the child from trying to communicate. Or the other extreme can happen: because the child lacks experience in using language to express himself, he just cries when he wants something. For the sake of "peace and quiet" he will get it without having to say what he wants. The problem starts when the pampering stops. What has happened is that the child honestly does not know how to say what he is thinking. He has not been given enough opportunities to use spoken language so he is frustrated and you are frustrated.

The normal blind child, like the sighted child, begins to vocalize at eight weeks; he squeals with pleasure and talks when spoken to at 12 weeks; he says syllables like ba, ka, da at 28 weeks; he may say one word with meaning and imitate sounds at 48 weeks; and he may have two or three meaningful words in his vocabulary by one year of age. After this age, language development slows down. For example, he may start to repeat his words without understanding them fully. At about 16 to 18 months he may forget some of the words already learned. At this age he is attracted to sounds, and will imitate the sounds of familiar objects like cars and airplanes as well as the voices of people he knows. The blind child will learn to speak normally but it may take him a longer period of time than the sighted child.

Following are a variety of ways in which blind children can be helped toward understanding language:

1. Make sounds meaningful to your child by relating them to his experiences. For example, after you shake a rattle, put it into his hand and shake it again so that he learns to make the connection between the rattle and the sound it makes.

2. Talk with your child when you are feeding, bathing and playing with him. He will begin to understand words before he is able to use them if you tell him what you are doing as you do it.

3. Keep meaningless noises and speech, such as the constant playing of the radio or television, to a minimum so that he does not "tune out" all sounds.

4. As your child takes his toys out of the toy box, name them for him.

5. Move around the house with him, touching doors, tables, chairs, etc., telling him the names of these objects.

7. Once he knows the names of a large number of objects, teach him some action words or verbs. Examples are: give, go, take, push, pull, want.

8. One way to get your child to speak is to ask a question that he must answer if he is to get something he wants, e.g., "Do you want milk or juice?" Do not give him anything until he answers. Then give him just a little so that he will have to ask for more if he wants more.

9. Ask friends and family to talk directly to your child instead of asking you what he wants.

10. Try to avoid using phrases like "put it there" or "put it here." Your child will not know where *here* is or *there* is; he may not even know what *it* is.

11. Encourage him to ask questions.

Once your child can talk you will have to give him opportunities and topics to talk about. Try talking about whatever is going on at the time. If you are dusting, give him a rag and have him tell you what it is like to dust. You can do the same thing with most of your household chores. He can help you do the dishes or get the clothes ready for the wash. This will make it unnecessary for him to ask you every five minutes, "What are you doing now, Mom?"

Have make-believe conversations. You play the part of other people in his life: his grandmother, a friend, a storekeeper. This will give him practice communicating, making it more likely that he will talk more readily with these people when he meets them.

Nursery Rhymes

Your child will love all the classic nursery rhymes. Try to act out the lines. For example, "Jack jumped over the candlestick"—take a big jump while holding your child's hand. A familiar story or nursery rhyme will often encourage a child to speak if you stop suddenly before the last word, "Jack and Jill went up the _____" or "the Papa Bear said "Who has been sleeping in my _____?"

Sometimes you may wonder which stories are good for visually impaired children. Any story which you take the time to relate to your child has value because you are spending the time together.

Some children will sing when they are reluctant to talk. The tune to "Here We Go Round the Mulberry Bush" can be used with many words—"this is the way we brush our teeth, wash our hands and go to bed."

Anything which provides your child with the opportunity to speak will help him to become a friendly person who can talk to anyone.

Seeing

Do not eliminate words like "look" and "see" from your vocabulary or else you may have some explaining to do, just as Joanie's mother did. Joanie was carrying water from the kitchen through the living room and out the front door to water the grass. After about ten trips, Joanie's mother said that was enough. After a few seconds, Joanie tip-toed past her mother with another pitcher of water. Her mother quickly asked Joanie where she was going with the water. "Did you hear me?" Joanie asked. "No," her mother replied. "Then how did you know what I was doing?" asked Joanie. It took a few minutes for the reply, but Joanie's mother then said: "I saw you."

It is important that your child learns about "seeing" and "looking." Explain that you do not have to hear or touch in order to see. It is helpful for your child to be able to understand this so that he can learn about his handicap. Remember your child does not know about concepts like "feels sorry for himself" or "pity"; try not to use them when you are teaching him about his visual handicap. Despite his handicap, he can learn to "see."

Reference

Barraga, N. *Visual handicaps and learning.* Belmont, Calif.: Wadsworth Publishing, 1976.

Chapter 7

Learning How To
Use Vision

Few people with impaired vision are totally blind. Some vision, even the ability to distinguish light from dark, is useful in providing important information. It is essential that you understand the nature and extent of your child's visual disability and that you learn how to help him utilize whatever vision remains. Ask his doctor or a vision specialist for suggestions on how to train your child to make optimal use of the vision he has. Glasses, magnifiers or other optical aids may be of help.

Problem of diagnosis. It is essential for you to realize that your child may have a visual impairment that is not readily apparent to you or your doctor. The story of Brian is a case in point: an outgoing four-year-old, Brian started nursery school with enthusiasm, but by the end of the second week, a drastic change had taken place. He withdrew completely from everyone, and reacted violently when asked to join a group for coloring or tracing activities.

Unknown to his parents or teacher, Brian could not see the lines on the paper clearly and he could not follow them with a crayon or a pencil. Rather than show everyone his "scribbles" he chose to protect himself by refusing to cooperate. After observing him closely for a while, his teacher realized that Brian was having a problem seeing what was on the paper. At her suggestion, his mother took him to an ophthalmologist who gave him a pair of glasses to help him focus better. With his new glasses Brian was able to color and trace like the other children, and became the happy, outgoing child he had been.

Young children do not realize that objects are blurred because they do not know how they are supposed to look. It is difficult to give thorough eye examinations to young children, particularly those under three years of age, because they are often unwilling or unable to cooperate fully. If you suspect that your child has a visual problem, you may want to contact the National Society to Prevent Blindness (see p. 39) (212) 684-3505, and request their "Home Eye Test." It is designed for parents to give to their preschool children in order to determine whether they should seek professional help. Some of the signs you should be on the alert for include crossed eyes, red or swollen eyelids, and eyes that water a lot. Take note if your child rubs his eyes often, shuts or covers one eye, tilts his head while looking at an object, or shows difficulty while doing work that is close to his face. Also be aware if he constantly blinks, stumbles or trips over small objects, or squints or frowns to see objects in the distance. Listen carefully if he complains about his eyes burning, itching or feeling scratchy; if he feels dizzy or sick after he has been doing work close to his eyes; or if he says he sees double images. If you notice any of these signs, make a note of when and how often and make an appointment to have your child's eyes checked by an ophthalmologist. It is critical that you do not delay because certain eye conditions like "lazy eye" or amblyopia are best corrected if treatment begins by age three.

Another indication that your child may have an eye problem is delayed development. You may notice that he is slow in achieving some of the basic skills of eating, toilet training, and dressing. However, while visual difficulties *may* account for such learning delays, it is also possible that the problem is attributable to other factors. It is extremely important that the reasons, whatever they may be, are identified early enough for appropriate intervention.

Problems of Definitions. All too frequently, definitions have a way of labeling children and thus limiting them. You, as parents, will hear professionals use many words to describe your child and his handicap. Always ask them to explain it in terms that you can understand. The following is a list of some of the words that they may use (Barraga, 1976)

Blindness.

This term refers to light perception (the ability to distinguish between light and dark) without projection (unable to determine the direction of a light source), or the total absence of vision.

Low vision (or visual limitation).

Refers to the inability to use vision effectively for a particular activity under ordinary circumstances. Adaptations in lighting, prescriptive lenses, optical aids, and special materials can improve visual functioning.

Visual acuity.

This refers to sharpness of vision and is expressed in terms of the distance over which a person can see an object clearly. The visually impaired person with 20/200 acuity, for example, sees at 20 feet what a person with normal vision sees at 200 feet.

Visual impairment.

This is a term used to describe loss of vision due to deviation in the structure or functioning of the tissue or parts of the eye, or of that part of the brain responsible for vision.

Visual perception.

This is the ability to understand and interpret meaningfully all information received from the visual sense. This process is really related more to an individual's learning capabilities than to the condition of his eyes.

Legal blindness.

This term refers to central visual acuity that does not exceed 20/200 or a visual field that is less than a 20° angle. It is used for administrative purposes, usually to determine eligibility for funds and services.

Suggestions for developing use of vision.

You should begin teaching your child to use his vision when he is still an infant. Begin by decorating his room with colorful and appealing objects within his line of vision: on the ceiling, inside his crib, on the walls closest to him. Select toys, mainly mobiles and rattles, that are brightly colored and make a noise when touched.

Once your child can crawl by himself, teach him how to get around. Explain that light comes from lamps and through windows. Show him how he can move toward the light, and that from there, he can find his way around the room. Window light is a good reference point for a young child to learn.

Introduce colors at an early age. Dress him in brightly colored clothes. Tell him as you dress him about the colors he is wearing. Let him experience color by finger painting and coloring with crayons. Talk about colors in relation to objects and experiences commonly associated with them: For example, the sky is blue, grass is green, and red means stop.

Teach him to use his sight as well as his sense of touch to determine size, shape, height, and weight of objects. Let him point to a square or circle without picking it up. Build towers of blocks together, and then ask him to knock down the shortest or tallest one. Teach him to compare objects by using his sight, such as how the little goldfish looks next to the angel fish in the fish tank. You will also be teaching him how to pay attention to visual details, a skill which is important to remembering people, places and things.

You may want to buy the shape toy made by the Tupperware Company. It has yellow handles that pull apart, letting the shapes drop onto the table or the floor. Using his eye-hand coordination, your child has to fit the correct shape with the correct hole.

When buying toys, look for ones that will require him to match parts, such as snap-on Lego blocks, domino blocks, or Edu-cards.

Playing games such as baseball or catch will train your child's eye to watch a moving target. Kickball will help him to develop eye-foot coordination. Being able to play these games will also increase his sociability among his peers.

Any kind of a home-made sorting box which requires him to identify things that look alike can teach him to use his vision. Reds, oranges and greens are good colors to use in these sorting games. For example, you could use differently colored buttons and ask him to sort them by color.

These activities are meant to give you some ideas of where to begin teaching your child to use whatever vision he has. They are merely a foundation on which you can build. Be creative and add as many activities as you can. What is important is that you keep your child active and interested. Encourage his participation, be enthusiastic about his attempts, praise him when he succeeds. Above all, keep in mind that this is a time for learning — learning through your gentle guidance and consistent directions — that he CAN SEE, IF HE USES HIS VISION!

Appendix

Where to Find Help

There are various local and state organizations that provide assistance with the training and education of children with visual handicaps. You may wish to call on schools, libraries, local service groups and medical associations for information and support services.

For a comprehensive list of organizations see the *Directory of Agencies Serving the Visually Handicapped in the United States*, published by the American Foundation for the Blind (see below).

Private Agencies

American Foundation for the Blind
15 West 16th Street
New York, New York 10011
(212) 620-2000

(A list of selected references for visually handicapped infants and pre-school children is available from AFB's M.C. Migel Library.)

American Printing House for the Blind
1839 Frankfort Ave.
Louisville, Kentucky 40206
(502) 895-2405

Alliance for Education and Rehabilitation of the Visually Impaired, Inc.
206 North Washington Street
Alexandria, Virginia 22314
(703) 548-1884

National Society to Prevent Blindness
79 Madison Avenue
New York, New York 10016
(212) 684-3505

Government Agencies

Bureau of Education for the Handicapped
2100 Regional Office Building #3
Washington, D.C. 20202
(202) 245-9661

Office for the Handicapped
330 C Street S.W.
Washington, D.C. 20201
(202) 245-6644

National Institutes of Health, National Eye Institute
Bethesda, Maryland 20014
(301) 496-2234

Audio materials that may be of interest to you include talking books and tape recordings. You may request this material, free of charge, once you fill out a registration form with the agency located nearest you. You may want to write to the following organizations for a list of titles that are available.

Your local library may be able to arrange for you to borrow talking books or other materials; contact them.

Division for the Blind and Physically Handicapped
1291 Taylor Street N.W.
Washington, D.C. 20542
(202) 802-5500

Recording for the Blind
215 East 58th Street
New York, New York 10022
(212) 751-0860

The following organization publishes books with braille on the left hand page, and the print on the right hand page—
Twin Vision Books
Western Publishing Co., Inc.
1220 Mound Avenue
Racine, Wisconsin 53404

Medical Research Organizations

Eye-Bank Association of America, Inc.
3195 Maplewood Avenue
Winston-Salem, North Carolina 27103
(919) 768-0719

Fight for Sight, Inc.
National Council to Combat Blindness, Inc.
41 West 55th Street
New York, New York 10019
(212) 751-1118

Parent Groups

Many states have parent groups that are organized to help you meet the daily challenges of responding to the needs of your son or daughter. You may want to contact them for further information.

Council for Exceptional Children
1920 Association Drive
Reston, Virginia 22091
(703) 620-3660
Contact this office to inquire about the magazine *Educational Parent* and any other important information that is related to having a young visually impaired child.

Child Development Center for Visually Impaired and
Blind Children of the New York Association for the Blind
11 East 59th Street
New York, New York 10022
(212) 355-2200 Ext. 101
Contact this Center for information about how a young child is educated; what materials they use; and what activities and exercises they recommend.

National Association for Parents of the Visually Impaired
P.O. Box 180806
Austin, Texas 78718
(512) 459-6651

Parent Network
1301 East 38th Street
Indianapolis, Indiana 46205
(317) 926-4142

Low Vision

Low Vision is a relative new field and much information has been written on it. You may want to write to the following Society and request information.

Low Vision Clinic
121 East 60th Street
New York, New York 10022

Bibliography

Abel, G. *Resources for teachers of the blind with sighted children.* New York: American Foundation for the Blind, 1957.

Adelson, E. & Fraiberg, S. Gross motor development in infants blind from birth. *Child Development,* 1974, 114-26.

Adkins, P. & Ainsa, T. An early stimulation program for visually handicapped infants and toddlers, *Education of the Visually Handicapped,* 1972, 9, 55-60.

American Foundation for the Blind. *A Step-by-step guide to personal management for blind persons* (2nd ed.). New York: Author, 1974.

American Foundation for the Blind. *Proceedings of the national seminar on services to the young child with visual impairment.* New York: Author, 1969.

Angus, H. Twenty questions about mobility, *New Outlook for the Blind,* 1969, 64, 214-218.

Apple, M. Kinesic training for blind persons: A vital means of communication, *New Outlook for the Blind,* 1972, 67, 201-208.

Association for the Education of the Visually Handicapped. *Selected papers: Fifty-second biennial conference, (1972).* Philadelphia: Author, 1976.

Axelrod, S. *Effects of early blindness.* (Research Series, No. 7). New York: American Foundation for the Blind, 1959.

Baird, A. Electronic aids: Can they help blind children? *Journal of Visual Impairment and Blindness,* 1977, 71, 97-101.

Barraga, N. *Aids for teaching basic concepts of sensory development.* Louisville, Ky.: American Printing House for the Blind, 1973.

Barraga, N. *Increased visual behavior in low vision children.* New York: American Foundation for the Blind, 1964.

Barraga N. *Teacher's guide for development of visual learning ability and utilization of low vision.* New York: American Foundation for the Blind, 1970.

Barraga N. *Visual handicaps and learning.* Belmont, Calif.: Wadsworth Publishing, 1976.

Barry, T. Environmental education for the blind, *Instructor,* 1977, 86, 106-107.

Barsch, R. *Enriching perception and cognition.* (Vol. 2). Seattle, Wash.: Special Child Publication, 1968.

Barsch, R. *The parent-teacher partnership.* Arlington, Va.: Council for Exceptional Children, 1969.

Bell, V. An educator's approach to assessing pre-school visually handicapped children. *Education of the Visually Handicapped,* October 1975, 84-89.

Benson, J. & Ross, L. Teaching parents to teach their children. *Teaching Exceptional Children,* 1972, 5, 32-35.

Berla, E. Effects of physical size and complexity on tactual discrimination of blind children. *Exceptional Parent,* 1972, 39, 120-124.

Berry, D. *A bibliographic guide to educational research.* Metucheun, N.J.: The Scarecrow Press, 1975.

Best, J. *Research in education.* Englewood Cliffs, N.J.: Prentice Hall, 1970.

Blos, J. N. Traditional nursery rhymes and games: Language learning experiences for preschool blind children. *New Outlook for the Blind,* 1974, 68, 268-275.

Borg, W. & Gall, M. *Educational research: An introduction.* New York: David McKay, 1971.

Brothers, R. Learning through listening: A review of the relevant factors. *New Outlook for the Blind,* 1971, 65, 224-231.

Brown, C. A new program for young blind children: A cornerstone for future service. *New Outlook for the Blind,* 1967, 66, 210-217.

Brown, J. Storytelling and the blind child. *New Outlook for the Blind,* 1972, **66**, 356-360.

Buell, C. Hiking aids physical, mental growth of blind children. *New Outlook for the Blind,* 1965, 59, 175-76.

Buell, E. *Physical education for blind children.* Springfield, Ill.: Charles C Thomas, 1974.

Buell, C. *Physical education and recreation for the visually handicapped.* Washington, D.C.: American Association for Health, Physical Education and Recreation, 1973.

Burlingham, D. Hearing and its role in the development in the blind child. *Psychoanalytic Study of the Child,* 1964, 19, 95-112.

Burlingham, D. Some notes on the development of the blind. *Psychoanalytic Study of the Child,* 1961, 16, 121-145.

Burlingham, D. Some problems of ego development in the blind child. *Psychoanalytic Study of the Child,* 1965, 20, 194-208.

Chaney, C. *Motoric aids to perceptual training.* Columbus, Ohio: Charles E. Merrill, 1968.

Chase, J. Developmental assessment of handicapped infants and young children: With special attention to the visually impaired. In Z. S. Jastrzembska (Ed.), *The effects of blindness and other impairments on early development.* New York: American Foundation for the Blind, 1976.

Clark, L. *International catalog: aids and appliances for blind and visually impaired persons.* New York: American Foundation for the Blind, 1973.

Cohen, J. The effects of blindness on children's development. *New Outlook for the Blind,* 1966, 60, 150-154.

Committee on the Education of the World Council for the Welfare of the Blind. *The Oslo Meetings: proceedings of the international conference of education of blind youth.* Watertown, Mass.: Eaton Press, 1957.

Connecticut Institute for the Blind in Hartford. Basic Concepts of Blind Children. *New Outlook for the Blind,* 1965, 59, 341-343.

Cook, D. *A guide to educational research.* Boston: Allyn & Bacon, 1965.

Corey, S. *Action research to improve school practices.* New York: Columbia University Press, 1953.

Corn, A.L. & Martinez, I. *When you have a visually handicapped child in your classroom: Suggestions for teachers.* New York: American Foundation for the Blind, 1977.

Coyne, P., Peterson, L., & Peterson, R. The development of spoon-feeding behavior in a blind child. *International Journal for the Education of the Blind,* 1968, 18, 108-112.

Cratty, B. *Perceptual and motor development in infants and children.* New York: Macmillan, 1970.

Cratty, B. & Sams, T. *The body image of blind children.* New York: American Foundation for the Blind, 1968.

Cutsforth, M. The preschool blind child at home. *Exceptional Children,* 1957, 24, 58-65.

Davidson, P. Some functions of active handling: Studies with blind humans. *New Outlook for the Blind,* 1976, 70, 198-202.

Davis, C. Development of the self concept. *New Outlook for the Blind,* 1964, 58, 49-51.

Dokecki, P. Verbalism and the blind: A critical review of the concept and the literature. *Exceptional Children,* 1966, 32, 525-530.

DuBose, R. Developmental needs in blind infants. *New Outlook for the Blind,* 1976, 70, 49-52.

Eichorn, J. Orientation and mobility for preschool blind children. *International Journal for the Education of the Blind,* 1967, 17, 48-50.

Englehart, M. *Methods of educational research.* Chicago: Rand McNally, 1972.

Felix, L. & Spungin, S. Preschool services for the visually handicapped: A national survey. *Journal of Visual Impairment and Blindness,* 1978, 72, 59-66.

Fleming, J. *Care and management of exceptional children.* New York: Appleton-Century-Crofts, 1973.

Flood, B. Better early than never. *Education of the Visually Handicapped,* 1977, 9, 36-40.

Flowers, W. *A sound source ball for blind children,* (Research Series Bulletin). New York: American Foundation for the Blind, 1968.

Foulke, E. The role of experience in the formation of concepts. *International Journal for the Education of the Blind,* 1962, 12, 1-6.

Fraiberg, S. An educational program for blind infants. *Journal of Special Education,* 1969, 3, 121-39.

Fraiberg, S. *Insights from the blind.* New York: Basic Books, 1977.

Fraiberg, S., Siegel, B. & Gibson, R. The role of sound in the search behaviour of a blind infant. *Psychoanalytic Study of the Child,* 1966, 21, 327-357.

Freedman, D. Smiling in blind infants and the issue of innate vs. acquired. *Journal of Child Psychology and Psychiatry,* 1964, 5, 171-184.

Froebel, F. The Small Child, In Spodeck (Ed.), *Early childhood education.* Englewood Cliffs, N.J.: Prentice Hall, 1973.

Fulker, W. *Techniques with tangibles.* Springfield, Ill.: Charles C Thomas, 1968.

Gesell, A. & Amatruda, G. *Developmental diagnosis: normal and abnormal child development.* New York: Hoeber, 1941.

Gesell, A. *The first five years of life: A guide to the study of the preschool child.* New York: Harper and Brothers, 1940.

Gesell, A., Ilg, F. & Bullis, C. *Vision, its development in infants and children.* New York: Hoeber, 1949.

Gillman, A. Handicap and cognition: Visual deprivation and the rate of motor development in infants. *New Outlook for the Blind,* 1973, 67, 309-314.

Goodenough, F. The importance of music in the life of a visually handicapped child. *Education of the Visually Handicapped,* 1970, 2, 28-32.

Gordon, I. *Baby learning through baby play: A parent's guide for the first two years.* New York: St. Martin's Press, 1970.

Gottesman, M. State development: A piagetian view. *New Outlook for the Blind,* 1976, 70, 94-100.

Groves, D. & Griffith, C. *Guiding the development of the young visually handicapped: A selected list of activities.* Columbus: Ohio State School for the Blind, 1969.

Gruber, K. & Moor, P. (Eds.). *No place to go.* New York: American Foundation for the Blind, 1963.

Halliday, C. & Kurzhals, I. *Stimulating environments for children who are visually impaired.* Springfield, Ill.: Charles C Thomas, 1976.

Halliday, C. *Visual impaired children: Learning development infancy to school.* Louisville, Ky.: American Printing House, 1970.

Harley, R. Programmed instruction in orientation and mobility for multiply impaired blind children.*New Outlook for the Blind,* 1975, 418-423.

Harley, R. Verbalism among blind children: An investigation and analysis *(Research Series Bulletin).* New York: American Foundation for the Blind, 1963.

Hart, V. *Beginning with the handicapped.* Springfield, Ill.: Charles C Thomas, 1978.

Hebb, D. *Organization of behavior.* New York: Wiley and Sons, 1949.

Hellmuth, J. *Exceptional infant.* New York: Brunner-Mazel, 1970.

Henderson, L. *The opening doors—my child's first eight years without sight.* New York: John Day, 1954.

Hill, E. & Ponder, P. *Orientation and mobility techniques: A guide for the practitioner.* New York: American Foundation for the Blind, 1976.

Higgins, L. *Classification in congenitally blind children: An examination of Inhelder's and Piaget's Theory* (Research Series 25). New York: American Foundation for the Blind, 1973.

Huffman, M. Symposium-self image: A guide to adjustment. A call for recreation. *New Outlook for the Blind,* 1961, 55, 86-89.

Illinois State Office of the Superintendent of Public Instruction. *Toys for early development of the young blind child. A guide for parents.* Springfield, Ill.: Author, 1971.

Illinois State Office fo the Superintendent of Public Instruction. *Preschool learning activities for the visually impaired child. A guide for parents.* Springfield, Ill.: Author, 1972.

Imamura, S. *Mother and blind child.* New York: American Foundation for the Blind, 1965.

Instructional Materials Reference Center. *Commercial aids that may be used or adapted for the visually handicapped.* Louisville, Ky.: American Printing House for the Blind, 1971.

Isaac, S. & Michael, W. *Handbook in research and evaluation.* San Diego: Robert Knapp, 1971.

Jan, J., Freeman, R., & Scott, E. *Visual impairment in children and adolescents.* New York: Grune and Stratton, 1977.

Jastrzembska, Z. *The effects of blindness and other impairments on early development.* New York: American Foundation for the Blind, 1976.

Johnson, O. & Blank, H. (Eds.). *Exceptional children research review.* Washington, D.C.: Council for Exceptional Children, 1968.

Kakalik, J. *Improving services to handicapped children with emphasis on hearing and vision impairments.* Santa Monica: Rand Corp., 1974.

Kirk, S. & Weiner, B. *Behavioral research on exceptional children.* Washington, D.C.: Council for Exceptional Children, 1963.

Kirk, S. *You and your retarded child: A manual for parents of retarded children.* Palo Alto, Calif: Pacific Books, 1968.

Kohler, I. *Orientation by aural cues* (Research Series Bulletin 4). New York: American Foundation for the Blind, 1964.

Kurzhals, I. Creating with materials can be of value for young blind children. *International Journal for the Education of the Blind,* 1961, 10, 75-79.

Kurzhals, I. Personality adjustment for the blind child in the classroom. *New Outlook for the Blind,* 1970, 64, 129-134.

Kvaraceus, W. & Nelson, H. *If Your Child Is Handicapped.* Boston: Porter Sargent, 1969.

Lairy, G. Problems in the adjustment of the visually impaired child, *New Outlook for the Blind,* 1969, 63, 33-41.

Lairy, G. & Covello, A. *The blind child and his parents: Congenital visual defect and the repercussion of family attitudes on the early development of the child* (Research Series Bulletin 25). New York: American Foundation for the blind, 1973.

Langley, E. Self image: The formative years. *New Outlook for the Blind,* 1961, 55, 80-81.

Larson, R. Teaching orientation to blind children. *Education of the Visually Handicapped,* 1975, 7, 26-31.

Love, H. *Parental attitudes toward exceptional children.* Springfield, Ill.: Charles C Thomas, 1970.

Lowenfeld, B. *Berthold Lowenfeld on blindness and blind people: Selected references.* New York: American Foundation for the Blind, 1982.

Lowenfeld, B. *Our blind children: Growing and learning with them.* Springfield, Ill.: Charles C Thomas, 1971.

Lydon, W. & McGraw, L. *Concept development for visually handicapped children: A resource guide for teachers and other professionals working in educational settings.* New York: American Foundation for the Blind. 1973.

Manley, J. Orientation and foot travel for the blind child. *International Journal for the Education of the Blind,* 1962, 12, 8-13.

McGuire, L. & Meyers, M. Early personality in the congenitally blind child. *New Outlook for the Blind,* 1971, 65, 137-143.

Miguel, M. & Cecialia, M. Helping the preschool blind child. *New Outlook for the Blind,* 1964, 63, 170-172.

Mills, R. Orientation and mobility for teachers. *Education of the Visually Handicapped,* 1970, 2, 80-82.

Moor, P. *A blind child can go to nursery school.* New York: American Foundation for the Blind, 1952.

Morris, R. A play environment for blind children. Design and evaluation. *New Outlook for the blind,* 1965, 15, 17-20.

Napier, G., Kappan, D. L., Tuttle, D. W., Schrotberg, W.L., & Dennison, A. L. *Handbook for teachers of the visually handicapped.* Louisville, Ky.: American Printing House for the Blind, 1974.

Norris, M., Spaulding, P., & Brodie, F. *Blindness in children.* Chicago: University of Chicago Press, 1957.

O'Brien, R. Early childhood services for visually impaired Children: A model program. *New Outlook for the Blind,* 1975, 69, 201-206.

Olson, M. *Guidelines and games for teaching efficient braille reading.* New York: American Foundation for the Blind, 1981.

Omwake, E. & Solnit, A. It isn't fair: The treatment of a blind child. *Psychoanalytic Study of the Child,* 1961, 76, 352-404.

Parten, C. Encouragement of sensory motor development in the preschool blind. *Exceptional Children,* 1971, 37, 739-741.

Peterson, C. Sharing your knowledge of folk guitar with a blind friend. *New Outlook for the Blind,* 1969, 63, 142-146.

Piaget, J. & Inhelder, B. *The psychology of the child.* New York: Basic Books, 1969.

Pittman, Y. An exploratory study of the eating habits of blind children. *New Outlook for the Blind,* 1964, 58, 264-267.

Pringle, M. The Emotional and Social Adjustment of Blind Children, *Educational Research,* 1964, 6, 129-138.

Rawls, R. Parental reactions and attitudes toward the blind child, *New Outlook for the Blind*, 1957, 51, 92-97.

Reger, R. (Ed.). *Preschool programming of children with disabilities.* Springfield, Ill.: Charles C Thomas, 1970.

Reichard, C. & Blackburn, D. *Music based instruction for the exceptional child.* Denver: Love Publishing, 1973.

Rogow, S. Perceptual organization in blind children. *New Outlook for the Blind*, 1975, 69, 226-233.

Rogow, S. Puppetry as an aid in language development. *New Outlook for the Blind*, 1965, 59, 272-274.

Rowen, B. *Learning through motivation.* New York: Columbia University Press, 1963.

Rubin, E. *Abstract functioning in the blind.* New York: American Foundation for the Blind, 1964.

Rutberg, J. Orientation and mobility in the urban environment: A form of future shock, *New Outlook for the Blind*, 1976, 70, 89-93.

Santin, S. & Simmons, J. Problems in the construction of reality in congenitally blind children. *Journal of Visual Impairment and Blindness*, 1977, 71, 425-429.

Scheffers, W. Sighted children learn about blindness. *Journal of Visual Impairment and blindness*, 1977, 71, 258-261.

Schleifer, M. Case history: My brother, he's blind. *Exceptional Parents*, 1973, 3, 31-34.

Scott, E. & Freeman, J. *Can't your child see? A guide for parents and professionals.* Baltimore: University Park Press, 1977.

Scott, R. *The making of blind men.* New York: Russell Sage Foundation, 1968.

Singer, R. *Motor learning and human performance.* New York: Macmillan, 1968.

Sokolow, A. & Urwin, C. Play mobile for blind infants. *Developmental Medicine and Child Neurology*, 1976, 18, 498-502.

Special Learning Corporation. *Readings in visually handicapped education.* Guilford, Conn.: 1978.

Spittler, M. Games for the development of pre-orientation and mobility skills. *New Outlook for the Blind*, 1975, 69, 452-456.

Spodek, B. *Early childhood education.* Englewood Cliffs, N.J.: Prentice Hall, 1973.

Stocker, C. *Listening for the visually impaired: A teacher's manual.* Springfield, Ill.: Charles C Thomas, 1973.

Stratton, J. *The blind child in the regular kindergarten.* Springfield, Ill.: Charles C Thomas, 1977.

Strelow, E. & Hodgson, R. The development of spatial sensing system for blind children. *New Outlook for the Blind*, 1976, 70, 22-24.

Swallow, R. Piaget's theory and the visually handicapped learner. *New Outlook for the Blind*, 1976, 70, 273-281.

Tait, P. Behavior of young blind children in a controlled play session. *Perceptual and Motor Skills*, 1972, 24, 963-969.

Tait, P. A descriptive analysis of the play of young blind children. *Education of the Visually Handicapped*, 1972, 4, 12-15.

Tait, P. The effect of circumstantial rejection on infant behavior. *New Outlook for the Blind*, 1972, 66, 139-149.

Tait, P. Play and the intellectual development of blind children. *New Outlook for the Blind*, 1972, 66, 361-369.

Taylor, B. *Blind preschool: A manual for parents of blind preschool children.* Colorado Springs: Industrial Printers of Colorado, 1974.

Toll, D. Should museums serve the visually handicapped? *New Outlook for the Blind*, 1975, 69, 461-464.

Toomer, J. & Brown, M. Learning through play. *New Outlook for the Blind*, 1965, 59, 24-26.

Travers, R. *An introduction to educational research.* New York: Macmillan, 1969.

Ulrich, S. *Elizabeth.* Ann Arbor: University of Michigan, 1972.

Van Osdol, B. *Vocabulary in special education.* Moscow: University of Idaho Research Foundation, 1972.

Vogel, M. Creating a toy for a blind child. *New Outlook for the Blind*, 1968, 62, 253.

Wardell, K. Parental assistance in orientation and mobility instruction. *New Outlook for the Blind*, 1976, 70, 321-325.

Wardell, K. Preparatory concepts in orientation and mobility training. *Education of the Visually Handicapped*, 1972, 4, 86-87.

Warren, D. *Blindness and early childhood development*. New York: American Foundation for the Blind, 1977.

Warren, D. Blindness and early development: Issues in research methodology. *New Outlook for the Blind*, 1976,70, 53-60.

Warren, D. Blindness and early development: What is known and what needs to be studied. *New Outlook for the blind*, 1976, 70, 5-16.

Webster, Richard. A Concept Developmental Program for Future Mobility Training. *New Outlook for the Blind*, 1976,70, 195-197.

Welford, A. *Skilled performance: perceptual and motor skills*. Glenview, Ill.: Scott, Foresman Co., 1976.

Welsh, R. & Blasch, B. *Foundations of orientation and mobility*. New York: American Foundation for the Blind, 1980.

Yeadon, A. *Toward independence: The use of instructional objectives in teaching daily living skills to blind persons*. New York: American Foundation for the Blind, 1974.

Zok, J. *Instructional manual for blind bowlers*. Washington, D.C.: American Association of Blind Bowlers, 1970.

Zweibelson, I. & Barg, C. Concept development in blind children. *New Outlook for the Blind*, 1967, 61, 218-222.